Practical
Cinematography

D0078139

PITTSBURGH FILMMAKERS LIBRARY
10003880

PITTSBURGH FILMMAKERS
477 MELWOOD AVENUE
PITTSBURGH, PA 15213

DATE DUE			
11-14			
2-5-09			
2-25-09			
3/7/14			

TR 850 .W53 2005
PRACTICAL CINEMATOGRAPHY
Wheeler, Paul
film, production: cinematography

Dedication

To the memory of my father

Leslie J. Wheeler

who taught me the

Principles of Cinematography

Practical Cinematography

Second edition

Paul Wheeler BSC FBKS

AMSTERDAM • BOSTON • HEIDELBERG • LONDON • NEW YORK • OXFORD
PARIS • SAN DIEGO • SAN FRANCISCO • SINGAPORE • SYDNEY • TOKYO
Focal Press is an imprint of Elsevier

Focal Press
An imprint of Elsevier
Linacre House, Jordan Hill, Oxford OX2 8DP
30 Corporate Drive, Burlington MA 01803

First published 2000
Reprinted 2001
Second edition 2005

Copyright © 2000, 2005 Paul Wheeler. All rights reserved

The right of Paul Wheeler to be identified as the author of this work has
been asserted in accordance with the Copyright, Designs and Patents
Act 1988

No part of this publication may be reproduced in any material form
(including photocopying or storing in any medium by electronic means
and whether or not transiently or incidentally to some other use of this
publication) without the written permission of the copyright holder except
in accordance with the provisions of the Copyright, Designs and Patents
Act 1988 or under the terms of a licence issued by the Copyright Licensing
Agency Ltd, 90 Tottenham Court Road, London, England W1T 4LP.
Applications for the copyright holder's written permission to reproduce
any part of this publication should be addressed to the publisher

Permissions may be sought directly from Elsevier's Science and Technology
Rights Department in Oxford, UK: phone: (+44) (0) 1865 843830; fax:
(+44) (0) 1865 853333; e-mail: permissions@elsevier.co.uk. You may also
complete your request on-line via the Elsevier homepage (www.elsevier.com),
by selecting 'Customer Support' and then 'Obtaining Permissions'

British Library Cataloguing in Publication Data
A catalogue record for this book is available from the British Library

Library of Congress Cataloguing in Publication Data
A catalogue record for this book is available from the Library of Congress

ISBN   0 240 51962 0

For information on all Focal Press publications visit our
website at: www.focalpress.com

Printed and bound in USA

Working together to grow
libraries in developing countries

www.elsevier.com | www.bookaid.org | www.sabre.org

ELSEVIER   BOOK AID
            International   Sabre Foundation

Contents

Preface

When I joined the BBC in the 1960s as a trainee projectionist, I was the youngest trainee at that time. I was lucky enough to be entering a world which offered the best possible training for any aspiring film-maker. As I progressed through the grades, becoming eventually one of the six senior film cameramen before leaving to go freelance, I enjoyed a substantial amount of practical and theoretical training. That training no longer exists – indeed, the BBC Film Department no longer exists, and you cannot get that training anywhere now.

One of the most enjoyable aspects of being a Director of Photography is the opportunity to shoot a wide variety of work. Recently, for instance, I have shot three hours of 35 mm, three hours of Super 16, two hours of Digi Beta, and a one-hour television studio opera and three hours of High Definition – HD. This variety, combined with the opportunity to work with different producers, directors, actors and crew, makes ours one of the most stimulating jobs I know.

Some years ago, I was asked to stand in as Head of Cinematography at the National Film and Television School. Since then, I have repeated that enjoyable position. I have also been asked to take various short courses in a variety of training establishments, something I always enjoy doing, if I am not shooting.

Since I wrote the first edition of this book, I have had a great deal of feedback from readers and this has led me to a greater understanding of their needs. Therefore, this new edition has a more defined purpose – to lead a student or someone in a lower grade than the DP to gain the knowledge to be able to aspire to that most wonderful of jobs – the Director of Photography.

This edition, therefore, starts with the definition and description of the tasks of the DP and goes on to describe all the necessary technical knowledge one might need to get a commission as a DP.

As I have always found it easier to explain theoretical principles using diagrams and pictures in preference to relying on words alone, this book contains a large number of figures. Indeed, for some of the sections, I prepared the figures first and then wrote the text afterwards.

In this new edition there are some added chapters, a complete reorganization of the structure of the book, together with many added illustrations, including over 20 photographs.

Paul Wheeler

About the author

Paul Wheeler has a wealth of practical experience as a cinematographer combined with wide experience as a highly respected trainer. After 25 years with the BBC, by the end of which he was one of only six senior film cameramen out of a total of 63 DPs employed there at that time, he left to go freelance.

In the years since leaving the BBC, Paul has had a flourishing career which has bought him many awards both in the UK and internationally. In between films, he has stood in as Head of Cinematography at the National Film and Television School a number of times and still takes master classes there. He was also Head of Cinematography at the Royal College of Art. Paul regularly teaches at the New York Film Academy in London (www.nyfa.com) as Tutor in Advanced Cinematography and runs courses at the National Short Course Training Program (www.nftsfilm-tv.ac.uk).

While still maintaining a busy shooting schedule, Paul has decided to spend more time writing and teaching in an effort to improve the quality of knowledge among young Directors of Photography.

Paul's other two books, both published by Focal Press, are *Digital Cinematography* and *High Definition and 24P Cinematography*.

Acknowledgements

Everyone listed here has made significant contributions to the writing of this book. They are listed in no particular order.

Paul Boutle, Brian Newman, Rowland Little, Mike Salter, Garry Willis, Julian Morson, Suzi Jackobson, Renos Louka, Mike McHugh, Alan Piper, Peter Swarbrick, Tony Harcourt, Paddy Seale, Roger Crittenden, Deanne Edwards and Steve Shaw.

All the illustrations are the copyright of the author with the exception of:

Figure 5.5, which is the copyright of Cooke Optics Limited.
Figure 17.2, which is the copyright of KJM Consultants.

Introduction

The premise I used to write this, the second edition of this book, is different from that I used for the first edition.

Now I have set out my stall in the first chapter, in which I describe the tasks and responsibilities of the Director of Photography. The rest of the book then tells you how to gain the skills and knowledge you will need, one day, to get your first job as a DP.

You may not use some of the knowledge contained herein on a day-to-day basis on the set, but if you have it somewhere at the back of your mind you will be a much more proficient DP.

I have also been very conscious of the skills needed in the positions leading up to the DP's job; hence, there are chapters on focus pulling, circles of confusion, etc. to enable you to become a very competent 1st AC or focus puller. There are chapters on composition and related matters to take you further on to becoming the camera operator.

Then there is all you will need regarding lighting ratios, exposure meters and what your crew can do for you, together with chapters on the laboratory, grading or timing and digital intermediates that will take you finally to the DP's position.

Part One
People

1
The Director of Photography – an overview

I imagine most people buying this book will have aspirations to become a Director of Photography (DP), and therefore I will start the first chapter by discussing and defining the roles and tasks required of the DP. The rest of the book will take you through the necessary knowledge you will need to acquire before you can use the title DP.

The DP is the senior head of department (HOD), whose level of responsibility and depth and breadth of tasks may only be equalled, and then only on a very big picture, by the production designer. All the HODs work to the director.

The prime job of the DP is to create the visual mood of the film and this is primarily achieved by the use and control of light. This, to my mind, is the most exciting part of the job. Even on a simple exterior, the DP will be making judgements that can materially affect the way the audience will perceive the message the script, the direction and the characters the actors are playing is interpreted.

My firm belief is that to bring the most to a movie and also to get the maximum enjoyment from shooting it, the DP must get the preparation right. Nothing, to me, affects the outcome more significantly, not even your talent.

The DP's responsibilities

The DP will be responsible for many things and I am not going to list all of them here. If you would like to peruse a detailed list, the *American Cinematographer* gave a full and exhaustive list in their January 2003 edition and that took three pages of small type. Nevertheless, here are the actions and responsibilities I consider most relevant and most likely to occur; use them as a check list if you will.

In early pre-production

- The first and most important matter is to discuss, in depth and possibly on many occasions, the script with the director until you are both in complete agreement as to the overall look of the film.
- In order to achieve the above, you will have had to have read the script several times, often between your meetings with the director. Early on, you should have made some decisions as to the ebb and flow of the emotional content of the script, so that the mood of your photography will be sympathetic to the story needs.
- During your discussions with the director, the production designer will be having similar discussions and it is most important that the DP and the production designer do not go off in different directions. Very early on, you and the production designer will need to keep in close contact; this will necessitate some meetings with just the two of you and some with the director present.
- Stay in close contact with the locations department and scout, or recce, proposed locations as early as possible.
- If sets are to be built, then you will need to keep a close eye on the progress of the plans, as simple changes that might mean nothing to others can materially affect the ease with which you will be able to light and shoot the necessary scenes. This primarily relates to the size of the sets and their positioning within the studio.
- If the director wishes to work with storyboards, you should keep in close contact during their creation. A good storyboard artist can be one of your greatest allies during pre-production. If the director prefers not to work with a storyboard artist, perhaps through personal preference or even budgetary restraints, a storyboard from the director, even if only drawn as stick men and women, can still be a useful tool, especially if the director does not have the most wonderful 'picture' imagination. Do not take this comment as in any way derogatory; if that director has hired the DP for their visual imagination knowing it will complement theirs, that DP might very well enjoy making a more significant contribution to the movie in question. But remember to let the director make it their own. Don't tell everybody it was your idea; subtlety gets you hired more often.
- Come up with preliminary lighting plots as early as you can so that you can give the lighting company an idea of what you will be needing, and by assessing the number and type of lamps you will need the production office can get provisional lighting budgets organized.
- You will need to nominate your technical crew, as well as choose your film laboratory and equipment suppliers.

Close to shoot preparation

- Approve with wardrobe department all the colours and textures they are intending to use.
- Check any specific make-up requirements such as prosthetics, etc.
- Visit all sets that are still under construction together with the production designer and the construction manager.
- Visit sets with the production designer when construction is finished to approve colours and textures.

- Work with the assistant directors to formulate workable schedules and remind them of any scenes that are time specific due to sun position or tides, etc.
- Formulate your film stock breakdowns and your Technical Diary. See Chapter 2 as to how to do this.
- Attend all readings, run-throughs and off-set rehearsals. These may be the first time you get to see your artists in the flesh and your pre-visualization, from now on, will include the faces you will be photographing rather than your interpretation before they were cast.
- Establish that your shooting crew has amassed all the equipment you have ordered and that they are satisfied that their testing has been successful.
- Make contact with your laboratory, check who will be your daily contact and who will be grading (timing in the US) your rushes (dailies in the US). Your rushes or dailies are the first print ever struck from the camera negative and can be extraordinarily enlightening, especially early on in the shooting of a movie. Establish with your lab contact the processes you will require and ensure that they are fully aware of the look you are going for.
- Shoot and approve any tests you want to carry out, such as emulsion tests, wardrobe colour tests, make-up and prosthetics tests.
- Finalize lighting plans and communicate them to the gaffer.

During shooting

- Get a laboratory report as early as possible.
- Watch the rehearsals, or block-outs, of the scene to be shot.
- Devise and agree with the Director the shots required for the upcoming scene.
- Agree the most convenient shooting order with both the director and the first assistant director (1st AD).
- Ensure your lighting plan has been carried out to your wishes; confirm the stop to the first assistant camera (1st AC or focus puller).
- Work with the 1st AD on background action. This may depend on the union agreements with the background artists; it is common in the UK that the 1st AD and the DP may direct background artists without putting up their daily rate, but if the director gives them instruction they will earn significantly more for their day's work. Check the agreement with the production office.
- Give camera set-ups to your camera operator and confirm these with the director.
- Set any additional cameras for stunts, etc.
- At the end of each scene, confirm with the director that you have sufficient and appropriate shots to have adequately covered the scene. Advise the director as to additional shots if you think the editor may need them.
- Make sure that still photography and, if on set, the EPK (Electronic Press Kit) crew have all the materials they need. This is often overlooked, but to the DP it can be vital that all the pictures generated on set are as good as the DP's pictures. Bad publicity photographs, still or moving, can seriously damage a DP's reputation.
- Last thing at the end of the shooting day, confirm tomorrow's scenes with the director and the 1st AD.

- If the director wishes, discuss tomorrow's work.
- Check and approve call sheets for the following day before they are made official.
- Check if any of the junior members of your crew wish to ask you questions about the day's shooting in order to help their career development.

Post-production

- Time, or grade, any early trailers that may be being constructed.
- Check any EPKs to make sure they are of sufficient technical quality.
- Approve all effect or composite shots before they become part of the final cut.
- Time, or grade, the final cut.
- Attend digital intermediate (DI) grade if this route has been chosen. For further information on DIs, see Chapter 9.
- Approve or modify answer prints as necessary.
- Attend all transfers to tape versions.
- Supervise pan and scan recompositions.
- Supervise and/or approve all other deliverables – VHS, HD, SD, Pal versions, NTSC versions, etc.
- Look for the next picture to shoot.

2
The DP's preparation

Research

Many pictures require specific, detailed research, particularly if they are period pieces, or if the director asks for a certain style or look. With the run-up and preparation times currently being scheduled, however, there is often too little time to research your subject properly. It is therefore useful to accumulate a store of reference material or to have a good idea where such material can be found. This can help not just with preparing for a shoot, but also with an initial interview for a picture. Discussing a script you only received 24 hours earlier with a director who has been living with it for months can be a lot easier if you have an understanding of the script's context and can knowledgeably refer to images that relate to that script.

Regular visits to second-hand bookstores can provide a useful library of old picture books at very little cost. Several years before I needed them, I acquired a marvellous set of books covering the years of the Second World War almost entirely comprising of photographs taken at the time with minimal captions; there is a book for each year.

Some five or so years later, I was asked to shoot a picture which opened with men in a train returning from the Dieppe raid of 1942 with flashbacks of the men being rescued from the waters along the French coast. My set of books provided pictures of men actually in oil-covered water being picked out of a life raft after that raid, a picture of a woman waiting for a train containing survivors of that raid and one of people using an underground station as a bomb shelter. All these scenes were scenes in the script I had been offered and I was able to base my interpretation of the script on them.

While it is the DP's job to interpret the script and the director's vision of that script, it is an immense help if you can base your imagined pictures on reality – it brings a greater believability to the finished film.

Old photographic books are useful (as well as quite fun) to collect, as are books of fashion photographs. With old photographs it is often as useful to imagine why the picture is shot and styled in a certain way, as this puts one's thinking into the mind of the original photographer and you can begin to feel more of the mood of the times.

Nowadays, there are even books published on specific times. I have an excellent book, *The Golden Years*, a celebration of an Edwardian summer – I haven't made the film to go with it yet but its time will come.

Art books are a favourite starting point, especially of directors. When we made the BBC film *The Dark Angel* based on the book *Uncle Silas* by Sheridan Fenau, the director, during pre-production, showed me many pictures of Victorian paintings as references for various scenes. Once the shoot started, he preferred not to show me any photocopies of reference pictures he had in his script, as he did not want to inhibit my original thinking at that stage.

While touching on the subject of photocopying, it is important to be aware of the copyright on the original, be it pictures or words. Most large companies have bought a buy-out licence for limited copying, but if either they or you don't have legal access to the material you may find yourself in trouble.

The painter I, and I imagine all cinematographers, get asked to emulate most is Vermeer. Not easy, but it can be done. I was once asked for a Frans Hals look, but persuaded the director against that because the film was destined for television and there would have been so much black on the screen the actors might have become unrecognizable. Frans Hals' pictures require contemplation and television cutting rates give no time for that. Suggesting we shot another movie with reference to Edward Hopper was a brave move but I think we pulled it off. One very large lamp to give a single, crisp, shadow across the set and a light overall fill, together with careful location finding, was a good start. I just pray nobody ever asks for a Jackson Pollock!

Making up your own scrapbooks is an excellent way to accumulate images and enables you to add pictures from newspapers and magazines to your collection. Keep faces, buildings, events and all the rest in separate scrapbooks to enable easy reference. The very nature of these books is random, as pictures will be added in acquisition order, but this offers a definite advantage for, when I am stuck for an image to work from, just flicking through a couple of scrapbooks will as often as not start my mind off down an interesting path – not necessarily from a particular picture, but somehow the randomness fires up ideas and unlocks my visual imagination.

Preparing for a shoot

The recces or scouting

The recce, the English colloquial abbreviation for reconnoitre, or scouting as Americans call it, comes in two parts. Recceing with the director and/or the location manager some time prior to principal photography is usually productive and enjoyable. The technical recce, which usually occurs just a week or two before the shoot commences, where the DP has to finalize all the technical requirements, is usually straightforward hard work.

Recceing with the director and other department heads is a most creative process. It is the time, if you haven't worked together before, to get to know each other and understand each other's visualization of the film. At this stage there is often, still, a choice of some of the locations.

to be used and making the decisions together, helped by the location manager, is a valuable investment in the look of the film.

There will be much discussion on a director's recce as to costs and facilities needed for the various scenes. One should make the director aware of scenes that may require out of the ordinary equipment or labour. It is not uncommon for the director and the DP to discuss the value to the story of individual scenes as this relates to their costs, and make sure they are spending the budget on the important scenes rather than, as can happen, find they are spending huge amounts of cash to solve problems on scenes that do not necessarily warrant that investment.

Only when you have seen the primary locations can you start to put the images together in your mind. I often ask for photocopies of the leading actors' publicity photographs before the recce, so that I can put faces into the rooms and spaces.

I find the technical recce perhaps the hardest and most intense part of the film-making process, for in just a few days I must finalize all the technical requirements, agree with my gaffer as to the logistics of every location and ensure that all the equipment suppliers, and the production office, are aware of the call-off of equipment for the next several weeks.

All the other departments will be bringing you their problems, where they impact on your own, during these few days. Decisions made now must be of the highest quality, as a poor judgement now will come back to haunt you in several weeks' time.

It is for these reasons that I make the most thorough preparations and produce the lists discussed below.

The DP's preparation

As schedules get tighter and budgets decrease, perhaps the most effective way a cinematographer can reclaim lighting time on the set is to invest time in preparation. Without good preparation, too much time on set will be spent answering unnecessary questions and trying to steal time to make arrangements for upcoming shooting days, which are not, as yet, fully organized. Thus, with good preparation, a DP's time can be better deployed.

The most effective way of releasing time is to publish, before the first day of principal photography, a series of documents that allow anyone connected with the necessary arrangements to quickly, and easily, refer to the DP's requirements and make their contribution without further reference to the cinematographer.

Two things need to happen for this to be without trauma and to be effective. Firstly, the cinematographer has to give the time to the project. Secondly, they have to have a system in place to produce the documentation efficiently.

If you are comfortable using a computer, then things are easier. One thing computers are exceptionally good at is repeat business. Once you have generated a list they seem to positively revel in your ability to make changes to that list and to deliver a new version very quickly.

My greatest ally in this important area of efficiency is a palmtop or laptop computer. I used to use a Psion but these are no longer made, so now I store all my contacts, which at the last count numbered nearly 500, in my Palm and do all the lists and data for the shoot on a Toshiba laptop, which is powerful enough to be my main computer. I don't own a desktop. A modern laptop is all I need these days; indeed, this and my other two books were all written on a series of Toshibas, including the making of all the illustrations. Both my Palm and my Toshiba contain all this, together with an enormous database of just about every technician with whom I have ever worked.

Three words of warning: if you decide to work up your data for a picture on a laptop, make regular backups. I know it seems obvious but it is essential. Also, make sure the computer is insured; unfortunately, it is almost impossible to get insurance on the data contained on the hard drive so, again, it is your responsibility to make those backups. The production you are currently working on may be kind enough to cover it, but it is best to have your own insurance for, if not, fate may just decide it is going missing the day after you come off the company insurance.

If you do not want to use a computer, the alternative is to use a check-box list. Here you carefully write out your lists with just about everything you could possibly ever need on any production with a check-box against every entry. For each new production, you photocopy your original list and then just mark the items you require on this occasion.

There are four publications I provide the production with, all serving a different purpose:

1   The camera equipment list
2   The lighting equipment list
3   The film stock breakdown
4   The technical schedule.

In order to discuss the use, importance and preparation of these documents, I will refer to just one film, *Neville's Island*, a feature-length film shot in England for prime-time television transmission. This format contains most of the problems associated with any film production. It is also valuable that all the lists come from the same production for, in many ways, they are interrelated.

The camera equipment list

The camera equipment list will probably be published twice. The line producer, or production manager, will usually ask the DP early on in the production run-up for a guess, or wish list, of the equipment that will be required as the basic kit in order to get competitive quotes from different suppliers. This does not take away the DP's right to nominate a preferred supplier.

It is important that this list is reasonable and not an 'if only I could have' list. At this stage of pre-production, one does not want to frighten the budget controllers with a foolish amount of equipment. It is more important to list a reasonable kit in order that comparative estimates of different suppliers' prices may be obtained.

Once the supplier has been chosen, the recce is over and a basic list can be decided upon, it is vital that you provide this new list as soon as possible. This is not only so that a firm quote can be obtained, but also, more important to the DP, to ensure that the chosen supplier can deliver all their requirements or, if they need to subcontract some equipment, they then have sufficient time to make the necessary arrangements.

Figure 2.1 shows copies of the camera equipment list as delivered to the production office of *Neville's Island* just after the technical recce. Not only is all the equipment very accurately detailed, but the assumed supplier is noted as these may differ for various parts of the kit. Each section is quite clearly marked and short-term hire, such as the second camera body for the time spent away from London, is clearly indicated.

This accuracy is important, as it is quite possible that someone in the production office may have to book the equipment while all the informed staff are out of the office. It is only fair to them that you have produced a list that can be read down a phone by someone who knows little about camera equipment. This is not only a kindness to them, but an insurance policy for the DP.

In addition, the page number and the full number of pages are clearly shown in the bottom right-hand corner of the page, and in the top right-hand corner the publication date is shown – this is very important. The DP will quite likely deliver a number of updated versions of the camera equipment list as the production nears the first day of principal photography. It is very important that anyone on the production who needs to refer to the list can easily see which is the latest version.

The camera equipment list, as illustrated, is exactly as written in my computer. These days computers are pretty compatible, so you should be able to plug into any office printer if you don't want the bother of carrying a small, portable, one. The DP can return from a recce and, say over lunch, print out various lists, etc. in order to have them ready for an after-lunch production meeting. This kind of organization is very much appreciated by the production.

The lighting equipment list

As with the camera list, in all probability the production office will need an early lighting equipment list in order to obtain comparative costings from differing suppliers. Unlike the camera list, where a close guess of the requirements can be made from reading the script, with the lighting list it is very difficult to give a reasonably accurate judgement of one's needs before having seen all the locations; nevertheless, a list to base budgets upon will be requested.

My gaffer and I usually solve this by offering a list from a previous film that had a similar script and schedule – this at least provides a starting point. This provisional list only needs to contain the lamps and will look roughly like the first page of Figure 2.2, but without the filters and consumables. The suppliers will be able to give a rough estimate from this, as all the accessories are fairly standard.

During the recce, my gaffer and I will be continually updating the list of the lighting equipment we will need to carry as the standard kit, together with a daily extras list that will eventually become part of the technical schedule described later in this chapter.

As soon as the technical recce is complete, my gaffer and I will sit down with my laptop and compile the full list of all the lighting equipment he will require. As I can never remember all the bits and pieces he likes to have, we will either modify a previous list of an

Camera Equipment   *"NEVILLE'S ISLAND"*   *@ 7th October*

Aaton XTRprod Camera Kit

Camera   *Supplier – Cine Europe*
Aaton XTRprod with video assist + 4 magazines all for super 16 and
with PL lens mount Extension viewfinder with leveler ring
2nd Aaton XTRprod with video assist – body only with
extension viewfinder and leveler ring from 3th Oct. to 27th Oct only

Zoom Lenses   *Supplier – Cine Europe*
Canon 7–63 mm T2.6 Zoom lens in PL mount
Canon 11.5–138 mm T2.5 Zoom lens in PL mount

Prime Lenses   *Supplier – Cine Europe*
All in Arri PL mount
8 mm Optex lens T1.9
12 mm Zeiss T1.3 High Speed Distagon
16 mm Zeiss T1.3 High Speed Distagon
25 mm Zeiss T1.3 High Speed Distagon

Telephoto Prime Lenses   *Supplier – P. W.*
180 mm Zeiss Sonnar T2.8 (Universal Mount)
300 mm Kinoptic T4 (Universal Mount)
500 mm Kinoptic T5.7 (Universal Mount)
Universal – PL mount adapter

Camera Accessories   *Supplier – Cine Europe*
2 × sliding base plates with 19 mm bars
Arri MB 16 4" production matte box with 4 × 4" filter slides +
1 × 4 × 6" filter slide
Clip on 4" Matte box for Distagons
Arri follow focus unit (manual)
Arri Lens control system (or Microforce as per David Hedges)

Video Assist Accessories   *Supplier – Cine Europe*
9" mains battery monitor
4" battery monitor
Trolley
3 × long & 3 × short BNC cables
2 × cable drums
4 × Heavy duty batteries

Filters   *Supplier – P. W.*
Standard Kit Includes:
4 inch Filters: 85, 85C, 0.9 ND. 2 × 85 ND6, Tiffen 812, Promist 1/4, 1/2, 1, 2, 3,
UltraCon 1, 2, 3, 4. 2 × Polar, Optical Flat. 0.6 & 0.9 ND Grads. No 1 Sepia
3 × 4" Filters: 0.3, 0.6, 0.9 ND Grads, 85B, 85C, 85BN6, 81EF, Tiffen 812.

Paul Wheeler   *Page 1 of 2*

Figure 2.1 Camera equipment list for *Neville's Island*

Camera Equipment   **"NEVILLE'S ISLAND"**   **@ 7th October**

3 inch Filters: 85B, 85C, 85, 85BN6, 81EF, FLB, 82C, 82B, Coral 6, 8, 10, ND6, ND9, LC1, LC2, 4 Point Star, Nos. 1 & 2 Diopters, Split Field Diopter.
Series 9 Filters: Plus 1 Diopter, 85B. Nets: Black Dior 10 Denier, Brown Silk, White etc.
Cokin Pro: Sunset 1 & 2, Grads: B1, B2, G1, G2. Tobacco grad, 6" Armored glass

Selection of gelatin filters to be charged @ cost of each as used

Grip Equipment   **Supplier – Cine Europe or Grip**
Super peewee Dolly
Doorway dolly
150 mm Arri Bowl "world cup"
3 way & 4 way Moy levelers
Paddle mount
Off set arm
50′ straight rail
Ladderpod
Low rocker
Bazooka
All usual grips "Toys"
3 × 8′ × 4′ boards and frames
2 × 4′ × 4′ boards and frames

Heads & Legs   **Supplier – P. W.**
Mitchell lightweight geared head – Moy fitting
Mitchell front box
Eyepiece leveler
Heavy duty carbon fibre tall legs – Moy fitting
Heavy duty carbon fibre short legs – Moy fitting
"Banjo" spreader
Ronford Fluid 7 head – with Moy & Arri bowl bases
Ronford Fluid 15 head – Arri bowl fitting
Ronford medium duty tall legs – Arri bowl fitting
Ronford medium duty short legs – Arri bowl fitting
Ronford dedicated spreader
Moy fitting to Arri bowl adapter
Shoulder Holder PRO hand held kit
Vinten Monopod

Waders for entire camera crew   **Purchase ??**

Please Note: Extra equipment needed on a daily basis is shown on the Technical Schedule

Paul Wheeler   *Page 2 of 2*

Figure 2.1 *continued*

Lighting List   **"NEVILLE'S ISLAND"**   *@ 7th October*

HMI

2 × 4 k MSR's
2 × 2.5 MSR's
2 × 1.2 ArriSun's
4 × 575 HMI's
2 × 200 MSR Battery Lights + Mains units
2 × Sungun battery lights
8 × Standard batteries + 1 × heavy duty battery
1 + Medium Daylight Bank Chimera for 1.2 ArriSun's with louvres

FLUORESCENT

2 × 4 bank Kino Flo's

TUNGSTEN

2 × 2 k Fresnel
2 × 2 k Blondes
4 × 800 w Redheads
4 × 1 k Pups
2 × Lee Zaps
8 × Mizars or Kittens
4 × Dedo lights
1 × Small Quartz Bank Chimera for Redheads
1 × Medium Quartz Bank Chimera for 2 k Blondes 3 × Atlas fittings – on TV spigots

PRACTICALS

Selection of tungsten household bulbs, clear & pearl
4 × No 1 Photofloods
4 × No 2 Photofloods
1 × Box 13 amp plugs

FILTERS & CONSUMABLES

1/4, 1/2 & Full Blue
1/4, 1/2 & Full CTO
0.3, 0.6 & 0.9 ND gel
Cosmetic Pink, Defusion Fl, F2 & F3, 3002 Rosco soft frost & Spun Glass etc.
Rosco Gold & Silver "Soft" reflector
Rosco silver/black scrim
Blackwrap

Paul Wheeler   *Page 1 of 3*

Figure 2.2 Lighting equipment list for *Neville's Island*

Lighting List   **"NEVILLE'S ISLAND"**   **@ 7th October**

STANDS

10 × Triple Lift
12 × Redhead/Blonde stands
10 × Flag stands + arms
2 × Low boy
3 × Double wind up
2 × High Rollers
2 × Double stand extensions

CABLES

125 amp extension – 500 feet
63 amp extension – 600 feet
32 amp extension – 10 × 100 feet + 10 × 50 feet + 5 × 25 feet
16 amp extension – 10 × 100 feet + 10 × 50 feet + 10 × 25 feet

MAINS DISTRIBUTION

2 × 125 Dist. box
2 × 63 Dist. box
4 × 32 Dist. box

JUMPERS & SPLITTERS

2 × 63a O/E
2 × 125 − 63
2 × 63 − 32
12 × 32 − 16
12 × 16 − 16
10 × 13 amp to 16 amp jumpers
6 × 32 amp open ends
6 × 4 way 13 amp
6 × 2 way or 1 way 13 amp
10 × 13 amp − 16 amp jumpers
8 × 16 amp male – chock block

Paul Wheeler   **Page 2 of 3**

Figure 2.2   *continued*

ACCESSORIES

2 × Long polecats
2 × Medium polecats
3 × Short polecats
2 × Doorway polecats
2 × Trombones
4 × Flat plate turtles
6 × Spigot reducers
10 × Magic arms
6 × "C" clamps
6 × "G" clamps – large
4 × Sash clamps
4 × Arri special clamps
2 × Pallet knives
Selection of 1/2 & 1 stop nets
Good selection of flags & charlie bars
2 × Large ulcers
2 × 4 × 4 foot reflector, hard & soft
6 × Mizar snoots & base plates
10 × sand bags
1 × Large ladder
1 × Zarge
1 × Medium steps
Paul's box of mirrors
Paul's "Mirror Box" for police lamps
1 × 10 foot scaf pole
2 × Big Ben
6 × Double barrel clamp
1 × Bag plastic zip ties
8 × Poly holders
4 × Frame holders
2 × 4 × 4' foot frames
12 × Safety chains
4 × 2 k In line dimmers
2 × Hanks of sash
2 × Rolls gaffer tape
100 × Crock clips
8 × Head covers
1 × Practical box – to contain 10 13 Amp plugs
1 × 12 × l2 foot Butterfly + Griflon & Silk + black net + white net
1 × 6 × 6 foot Butterfly + Griflon & Silk + black net & white net
6 × 8 × 4 Sheet of Black and White polly board

Paul Wheeler *Page 3 of 3*

Figure 2.2 *continued*

earlier production, or if the list required is radically different, he will simply dictate the new list to me and I will type it into the computer. This results in a list as shown in Figure 2.2, which shows the actual list used on my example film *Neville's Island*.

We then either fax this to the production office or deliver it the following morning. A copy is usually also sent directly to the lighting supplier. Some urgency is required at this time, as one is usually only a few days away from principal photography by the time the last location has been recced; final budgets need to be agreed and the supplier needs to make sure that all the equipment on the list will be ready and on the lighting truck.

Requirements for the generator and lighting equipment truck do not go on the lighting list. My gaffer makes these arrangements directly with the lighting company. The same applies to cherry pickers and towers; these will appear on the technical schedule together with any equipment required on a daily basis.

The film stock breakdown

Not long before filming starts, the DP will be asked what film stocks they will be using and what quantities they estimate they will use of each stock. I have found a simple and accurate way of doing this. If you refer to Figure 2.3 you can see the layout I use. Again, this is on my laptop using Microsoft Excel. The list is made in scene number order with, for my own reference, day or night, interior or exterior and a very brief description of the scene as a reminder. Then comes a column for the filters I expect to use and finally a column for each type of film stock I intend to use.

The film stock is shown as a figure which represents a decimal number of the length of the scene as obtained from a page count of the shooting script. So, for instance, halfway down the first page of Figure 2.3 you will find scene 11a, which is shown as being 5.3 pages long. A little further down, scene 21 is shown as only 0.8 pages long. By using decimals, in preference to fractions, it is easy to get the computer program to do all the arithmetic at the end of the lists.

At the bottom of the second page of Figure 2.3 you can see how the final amounts of film estimated to be required are arrived at. Firstly, one adds up each column of page counts. In this instance, 72.2 pages will be shot on Kodak Vision 200T and 36.8 pages will be shot on Kodak Vision 320T. Simple arithmetic will relate the total number of pages to the running time of the film; this is multiplied by the producer's estimate of the shooting ratio they have put in the production budget. By relating, proportionally, the page counts to the total rolls you expect to use, you come up with the number of rolls you will need for the whole production.

A copy of the stock breakdown is also put in the camera truck so that the focus puller and the loader can refer to the day's scenes and know which filters and stock the DP is expecting to use. The camera then comes on to the set with a 99 per cent chance of being loaded and set up correctly.

On a long production it is unusual to have all your stock delivered at the beginning of the production. The film can be kept in ideal conditions at the manufacturers and, if they know your estimated requirements,

Film Stock Breakdown   "NEVILLE'S ISLAND"   @ *7th October*

Scene	Day Night	Int Ext	Description	Filter	Stock 200 T	Stock 320 T
1	D	Int	Office	85B		1.4
2	D	Ext	Valley Road	Sepia		0.2
3	D	Int	Neville's Car	Sepia		0.3
4	D	Ext	Valley Road	Sepia		0.2
5	D	Int	Angus's Car	Sepia		0.4
6	D	Ext	Another Mondeo	Sepia		0.2
7	D	Int	Roy's Mondeo	Sepia		0.4
7a	D	Ext	Valley Road	Sepia	0.4	
8	D	I/E	Gordon's Mondeo	Sepia	0.6	
8a	D	Ext	Neville's Island	Sepia	0.3	
9	D	Int	Breakfast @ hotel	85B	0.7	
10	D	Ext	Hotel Grounds	85B	0.9	
11	D	Ext	Gordon's Beach	85C	1.5	
11a	D	Ext	Shingle Beach	85C	5.3	
12	D	Ext	Shrub Hill	85C	0.5	
13	D	Ext	Shrub Hill	85C	0.3	
14	D	Ext	Shrub Hill	85C	1.2	
15	D	Ext	Shingle Beach	85C	0.5	
16	D	Ext	Garlic Patch	85C	5.8	
17	D	Ext	Lookout Tree	85C	0.9	
18	D	Ext	Heart of the Island	85C	0.5	
19	D	Ext	Mud Beach	85C	1.6	
20	D	Ext	Shingle Beach	85C	3.4	
21	D	Ext	Lookout Tree	85C	0.8	
22	D	Ext	Shingle Beach	85C	9	

END OF PART ONE

Scene	Day Night	Int Ext	Description	Filter	Stock 200 T	Stock 320 T
23	D	Ext	Shingle Beach	85C	5	
24	D	Ext	Shingle Beach	85C	6.3	
25	D	Ext	Shingle Beach	85C	0.3	
25a	N	Ext	Lookout Tree/Cold Moon?	None	0.2	
			OR if "ON THE BLINK"	*SUNSET*		
26	N	EXT	Sleeping Patch	None		6.3
27	D	INT	Boardroom	None	1.3	
28	N	EXT	Sleeping Patch	None		0.6
28a	N	EXT	Disco Boat Beach	None		1.1
29	N	EXT	Heart of Island	None		0.3
30	N	EXT	Interior Island	None		1.6

END OF PART TWO

Paul Wheeler   *Page 1 of 2*

Figure 2.3 Film stock breakdown for *Neville's Island*

Film Stock Breakdown   *"NEVILLE'S ISLAND"*   *@ 7th October*

Scene	Day Night	Int Ext	Description	Filter	Stock 200 T	Stock 320 T
31	N	EXT	Gorse Patch	None		1.6
32	N	EXT	Bracken	None		4.3
32a	D	EXT	Shingle Beach	None	4	
33	D	EXT	Gordon's Beach/Shingle Beach	None	1	
34	D	EXT	Shingle Beach	None	1.6	
35	D	EXT	Gordon's Beach	None	0.3	
36	D	EXT	Shingle Beach	None	1.2	
37	D	EXT	Gordon's Beach	None	0.7	
38	D	EXT	Lookout Tree	None	2	
39	D	EXT	Shingle Beach	None	1	
39a	D	EXT	Shingle Beach	None	10	
NO 40						
NO 41						
42	N	EXT	Promontory	None		0.7
42a	N	EXT	Shingle Beach	None		3
NO 43						
44	N	EXT	Heart of Island (Roy's Tree)	None		4.3
45	N	EXT	Shingle Beach	None		3.4
46	N	EXT	Heart of Island (Roy's Tree)	None		0.4
47	N	EXT	HELICOPTER BEACH	None		4
48		EXT	Traveling Police Boat	None		2.5
49	N	EXT	Jetty, Lake	None		1.5
50	N	EXT	Empty Jetty	None		1.2

PAGE COUNT   72.2   36.8

TOTAL PAGES   109   Pages

90 Min Programme @ 12:1 ratio   108   Rolls

OVERALL STOCK REQUIREMENTS

	200 T	320 T
Kodak code	200 T	320 T
TOTAL Stock Required	73	36
First order prior to going to Lake District	40	20

Paul Wheeler   *Page 2 of 2*

Figure 2.3 *continued*

Technical Schedule   *"NEVILLE'S ISLAND"*   *@ 7th October*

October 1997
Mon 13   **TRAVEL to Lake District**
                    Cine Jib to travel
Tue 14   LAKE DISTRICT – Scenes: 2, 4, 6, 7a, 8, 3, 5, 7, 8a
                    Camera: Normal Kit + Scene 8a CINE JIB
                    Lighting: Normal Kit + 3 men
Wed 15   LAKE DISTRICT – Scenes: 16, 17
                    Camera: Normal Kit + **LADDERPOD** waders as above
                    Lighting: Normal Kit + 3 men
Thu 16   LAKE DISTRICT – Scenes: 19, 11a
                    Camera: Normal kit + 1 × **SPLASH BAG** + 6 dry suits
                    (in right sizes) + 6 Pairs Waders (in right sizes)
                    NB Cine Jib returns
                    Lighting: Normal Kit + 3 men
Fri 17   LAKE DISTRICT – Scenes: 38, move to 23
                    Camera: Normal Kit + Ladderpod + waders
                    Lighting: Normal Kit + 3 men
Sat 18   LAKE DISTRICT – Scenes: 24, 25
                    Camera: Normal Kit + Dry suits + waders
                    Lighting: Normal Kit + 3 men
Sun 19   LAKE DISTRICT – Scenes: 20, 22pt
                    Camera: Normal Kit
                    Lighting: Normal Kit + 3 men
Mon 20   LAKE DISTRICT – Scenes: 33pt, 35, 37, 11 unit move 42, 44pt, 44pt, 45pt
                    Camera Kit: Normal kit + **SPLASH BAG** + Dry suits + waders
                    2nd Camera for fireworks
                    CAMERA SAFETY BOAT
                    Lighting: Normal Kit + 3 men
Tue 21   LAKE DISTRICT – Scenes: 20pt, 24pt, 21, 25a **(at SUNSET if poss)**
                    Camera: Normal kit + Ladderpod
                    Lighting: Normal Kit + 3 men + **shutter box dimmer**
                    HEADLIGHT TORCHES
Wed 22   LAKE DISTRICT – Scenes: 10, 49, 50
                    Camera: Normal Kit + **second grip travels** for Scenes 28a & 49
                    Boomslang OR Giraffe **CRANE**
                    Lighting: Normal Kit + 3 men + 8 Atlas fittings + 6 Blondes + 70 feet
                    of festoons with 20 each red, yellow & blue 40 w bulbs + 2 extra men
                    SCAFFOLD TOWER FOR LIGHTING RIG

Paul Wheeler   *Page 1 of 3*

Figure 2.4 Technical schedule for *Neville's Island*

Technical Schedule   *"NEVILLE'S ISLAND"*   *@ 7th October*

Thu 23   LAKE DISTRICT – Storrs Hall Hotel – Scenes: 9,
8a (Disco Boat), 28pt, 48
Camera: Normal Kit + **2nd camera**
CRANE ON JETTY ??? Check Weight Loading
Crane returns tonight ???
Lighting: Normal Kit + 3 men + Festoons & battery light for
Disco Boat
(+ Disco lights from DESIGN)
SCAFFOLD TOWER FOR LIGHTING RIG

**PLEASE CHECK – if we don't see back to hotel then we can lose extra electricians & lights –
if we do I still need them**

Fri 24   *TRAVEL DAY – Return London*
Sat 25   *DAY OFF*
Sun 26   *DAY OFF*
Mon 27   **TRENT PARK** – Scenes 22pt, 32a
Camera: Normal Kit
Lighting: Normal Kit + 3 men + stove effect
Tue 28   TRENT PARK – Scenes: 12, 13, 14, 15, 18
Camera: Normal Kit
Lighting: Normal Kit + 3 men
Wed 29   TRENT PARK – Scenes: 26, 28
Camera: Normal Kit
Lighting: Normal Kit + 3 men
SMOKE IN TREES – from design
Thu 30   TRENT PARK – Scenes: 29, 30, 31, 32
Camera: Normal Kit
Lighting: Normal Kit + 3 men + 2 EXTRA men + 2 × 12 K HMI's +
2 × Gladiator stands + 4 × 1.2 Arrisuns
HEADLIGHT TORCHES
SMOKE IN TREES – from design
Fri 31   TRENT PARK – Scenes: 12, 13, 14, 44pt
Camera: Normal Kit – **LADDER POD + 2nd Camera
for Scene 44**
Lighting: Normal Kit + 3 men + 2 EXTRA men + 2 × 12 K HMI's +
2 Gladiator stands + 4 × 1.2 Arrisuns
HEADLIGHT TORCHES
SMOKE IN TREES – from design

Paul Wheeler   *Page 2 of 3*

Figure 2.4 *continued*

Technical Schedule   *"NEVILLE'S ISLAND"*   *@ 7th October*

November 1997

Sat 1   TRENT PARK – Scenes: 44pt, 46
               Camera: Normal Kit + 2nd Camera for fireworks
               Lighting: Normal Kit + 3 men + 2 EXTRA men + 2 × 12 K HMI's +
               2 × Gladiator stands + 4 × 1.2 Arrisuns + **Shutter box**
               HEADLIGHT TORCHES
               SMOKE IN TREES – from design
Sun 2   *DAY OFF*
Mon 3   HAWLEY LAKE – Scenes: 47pt, 47pt
               Camera: Normal Kit
               Lighting: Normal Kit + 3 men + CID Follow spot +
               HMI battery lamp for boat
               CHERRY PICKER bucket black draped to be "Helicopter"
Tue 4   HAWLEY LAKE – Scenes: 33pt, 34, 36, 42a
               Camera: Normal Kit + **HEADLIGHT TORCHES**
               Lighting: Normal + 3 men
Wed 5   HAWLEY LAKE – Scenes: 47pt, 47pt (Loc. TBC)
               Camera: Normal Kit
               Lighting: Normal Kit + 3 men
Thu 6   HAWLEY LAKE – Scenes: 39pt, 39a pt
               Camera: Normal Kit
               Lighting: Normal Kit + 3 men
Fri 7   HAWLEY LAKE – Scenes: 39a
               Camera: Normal Kit
               Lighting: Normal Kit + 3 men
Sat 8   PRIMETIME Boardroom Scenes 1 & 27
               Camera: Normal Kit + Black Artcard (from art Dep.) + Multi image
               rotating prism
               Lighting: Normal Kit + 3 men + 4 × 200 w MSR's + Star Burst
               projector + 1 K Profile follow spot + Cracked oil machine
               END OF FILMING!!!
Sun 9   *DAY OFF*

Mon 10   **RETURN GEAR & *WRAP* – not scheduled by production**

Paul Wheeler   *Page 3 of 3*

Figure 2.4 *continued*

your full order of just one batch number for each type of film can be put aside in their fridge and delivered to your production office on a weekly basis. This helps keep the film stock in prime condition.

The technical schedule

Using almost any diary program on your computer you can generate a very accurate daily list of all your requirements for the whole of a film. Figure 2.4 shows the technical schedule for the whole of the *Neville's Island* shoot. Before going on a recce, enter 'Camera: Normal Kit' and 'Lighting: Normal Kit' on all the shooting days. Then, enter your days off so that they show on the agenda; this gives you an entry for every day of the whole shooting period. Now, referring to the production's draft schedule, enter the scene numbers you are going to shoot on all the given dates.

Having prepared your agenda in this way as you go round the locations on the technical recce, all you have to enter are the changes from the normal kit.

Publish this technical schedule as widely as possible and as soon after the last recce as is humanly possible. Apart from having saved the first assistant director and the line producer a lot of effort, you have now made it possible for the production office, should location dates change, to easily track your extra requirements just by looking at the old date, seeing which scene number the equipment relates to, and posting the requirements to wherever the scenes move to in the new schedule as planning progresses.

By producing this kind of technical schedule you make it easy for the office to keep the production on track and you have created a situation whereby you will be bothered far less on the set as things change. Hence you get more time to do what you really enjoy – shooting the movie!

You might like to read Figure 2.4 bearing in mind the kind of story it might have been. Monday 20 October includes camera splash bag, second camera for fireworks and CAMERA SAFETY BOAT together with, on Monday 3 November, CHERRY PICKER bucket to be draped to be 'Helicopter'. It was a very interesting picture to shoot!

3
The camera crew

An overview

Before a camera crew is formed for any production, the DP will probably have had an interview with the director and the producer. Particularly in television, it is quite normal for them to interview perhaps three DPs before making their choice, even if there was a clear favourite right at the beginning. It is a fortunate DP who is well known enough to the director and producer to be asked to shoot their film without having to be interviewed.

Once the DP is confirmed they will start to look for their operator. Most DPs have a preferred operator with a second choice in mind in case the first is already booked on another production. It is quite acceptable for the director to have a significant input into the choice of operator as, in the UK at least, the director will often work very closely with the operator to choose and set up the shots. In America it is equally common for the operator to work solely with the DP. The DP will, if this is the director's preferred way of working, most probably have had several meetings with the director and design department to set the overall look of the film, and as the director and DP often travel together on an away job there is plenty of time for them to discuss finer points before they reach the set. If they are not travelling together it is usual to have a discussion about the next day at the end of the day's shooting or, if the director doesn't want to commit themselves, first thing in the morning, perhaps at breakfast.

Once the operator has been chosen they will be asked to nominate a focus puller and clapper loader. These appointments will always require the approval of the DP, the producer and probably the director.

The camera crew works in a very supportive way – that is, each grade is only as good as the support they receive from the colleague around them. The individual crew responsibilities from the trainee through to the DP are therefore as follows.

The trainee

Many years ago it was common to have a trainee on the crew. Restrictions to budget and the collapse of both the studio system

Figure 3.1 The cup bat

and large television stations then caused producers to be very reluctant to sanction the very small costs of having a trainee. Things have now improved for trainees for the curious reason that most directors now wish to work with video assist, and that facility comes with batteries, cables, monitor stands, etc. Providing the director does not want to record the video image, in which case a trained video technician is the answer, most producers now see the trainee as an economical way of having the video assist organized and kept running.

This is all very good news. I am currently working with two clapper loaders who started on my crews as trainees looking after the video assist. At least one end of the cable is attached to the camera and that ensures that a good and willing trainee will get much advice from the shooting crew. Keeping the shooting crew fed with tea, coffee and snacks is a marvellous way of ensuring they hire you next time. One of my loaders, when my trainee, somehow found time to run an espresso coffee machine two or three times a day. Adding the director to the camera crew as people he was happy to provide this service to has ensured a very successful transition to the next grade.

Recently, some clever person invented a marvellous device to help the trainee or clapper loader with the tea transportation problem – the 'cup bat'. Figure 3.1 shows this wonderful invention. It is made from half-inch-thick MDF or plywood. The unit carpenter, if talked to nicely, will usually happily make you one in a free moment. The holes are just the right size for a polystyrene cup to sit in and still sit about an inch proud of the surface. Kept in the set box if the trainee is busy, any member of the crew can grab it in a spare moment and get the camera crew a cup of tea. If we are shooting exteriors where I, as DP, am not always that busy, I am quite happy to grab the cup bat and do a tea run. The bat has nine holes: I can use one cup for sugar and a spoon and, having kept a cup for myself, endear myself to seven others on the shooting crew. Including the director and continuity in a tea run is a welcome gesture from the camera department.

The clapper loader (AC2 or 2nd AC)

From the focus puller's point of view, the most important part of the loader's job is to bring them just about every part of the camera they may need during the shooting day. The focus puller must never leave the camera, so the loader could be thought of as the legs of the focus puller. A good loader will have the camera car, or truck (in the UK even a seven-ton truck will usually be referred to as the camera car) very neatly organized with everything in its place and always in the same place so that it can be found quickly, even in the dark.

A good loader will learn to anticipate which pieces of equipment will be needed and when they will be needed; they will then be able to be standing by with all the parts needed before they are asked. Magazines will be adjacent as and when the camera is close to needing reloading and will be loaded with an appropriate film stock. All this must be done without cluttering the set; it is not an acceptable solution to have everything that might be needed very close to the camera. Too many people will get cross at continually tripping over the camera boxes and if you are working outdoors then the slightest amount of rain will cause dreadful panic as equipment is put away. Good anticipation is essential to being a successful loader.

These days, it is the loader's job to put marks on the floor, usually with different coloured camera tape, for both the artists' sake and the focus puller's, these marks not necessarily being for the same purpose. It is a good idea to dedicate a colour to each artist. A very useful gadget is a 'tape stick', as shown in Figure 3.2, this being a hexagonal piece of wood with a round handle on the end. Each face of the hexagon will have pre-prepared strips of camera tape stuck on top of each other, one face for each colour. If you fold back about one inch of each piece of tape, they will be easy to pull off in a hurry.

It is a good idea for the loader to have a single bag or box close to camera with just the small bits they will need together with the report sheets, so that any spare moment can be used to keep up to date without leaving the set. This box or bag can also be used to hold the clapperboard, the cup bat, the mark stick, etc. For interiors and guaranteed dry days, most loaders seem to have prevailed on a unit carpenter to make them a divided set box, as illustrated in Figure 3.3. This can be of any size, but I recently saw one made to fit exactly on a Magliner trolley the crew were using to bring essential kit closer to the set – very impressive.

If cleanliness is next to godliness, then all good loaders would deserve to go to Heaven. The inside of the changing bag or, on a big picture, the darkroom, which may be in the camera truck, should be immaculately clean and should be cleaned several times a day.

We have all seen a hair in the gate, shown on a lab report as an HIG. That little image, actually the shadow of a hair-like object, waving at us from the edge of the screen makes the shot unusable. Some hairs come with the film and are the product of the slitting, or sciving, process. Film is made in wide rolls and, after coating with the photographic emulsion, is slit into the required width – for motion picture negative 16 mm, 35 mm or 65 mm.

Any cutting process produces swarf – this is fine strands of the material being cut. In the case of film the base plastic cuts very cleanly, the emulsion itself not so well. Therefore, our hairs are sometimes fine pieces of emulsion swarf. In the manufacturing process great care is taken to reduce this problem to a minimum and vacuum removal processes are employed at every stage but, such is the nature of things, occasionally some hairs get through.

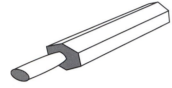

Figure 3.2 The tape stick

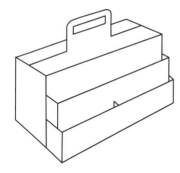

Figure 3.3 The set box

Because the film sometimes arrives at the loader's bag or darkroom carrying its little supply of hairs, loaders must be continually vigilant in their photographic housework. It has been known for a senior member of the camera crew, when passing the loader's bag, to turn it inside out and see how clean the corners are. It is no use them claiming they were going to clean it – it should have been clean. If, after a couple of inspections at the beginning of the picture, all is well and there are very few hairs appearing, then the loader will be left in peace.

Perhaps the most important responsibility of the loader is the paperwork. It is boring, but if the camera report sheet is not both legible and accurate it will be impossible to find the appropriate piece of negative come neg. cutting. Also, on most pictures the production office will be keeping a very close eye on the daily camera report sheets. This is for several reasons. The shot footage must be logged to see if the production is on budget in this area and they will want to know how much footage is being entered in the waste column. A reputation for good paperwork is the most common reason for a production office to approve the DP's nomination of a clapper loader. My loader keeps all the information regarding the lens, exposure, filters, etc. very neatly in a little book similar to a policeman's notebook. Should I need to refer back to any set-up, he then has the notes for the whole picture in his back pocket – very efficient. They also keep the notes on filters and the like to a minimum on the report sheet; this way, my techniques for achieving certain effects are not broadcast to too great an audience. Most DPs like to keep their ways of doing things within the crew, at least until the picture has been released.

At the end of every day the loader should check with the DP to see if there are any special notes they want entered on the laboratory report sheet. A typical, blank, report sheet is shown in Figure 3.4.

On a 35 mm picture it is the perceived wisdom in the production office that good loaders can save their salaries by intelligent juggling of which magazines are put on the camera when and thus reduce the amount of wasted film stock. A loader who is efficient in this area gets hired again.

The clapper part of the job is deceptively simple. I am appalled at how often a clapperboard is unreadable. It is vital that all the relevant information is on the clapperboard and that it is easily read. If you have ever tried to check the slate on a very blurred board that has started to leave the frame just before the clap is closed you will understand why.

Not only should the clapperboard be neat, but it must be put on film in the correct way. The board should be held very still as the clap stick is brought down and should then be held still for half a second after the clap; only then should it be removed. This will give the cutting room 12 frames of perfectly sharp board after the clap, which makes synching up the sound and picture very much easier. There is also a correct way of putting on a mute, or silent, board. The board should be held by the stick with the stick open and the board should be held only by this hand. This shows the cutting room that it is a mute shot as only an idiot would now clap the board on their own fingers.

Once, clapperboards were made wholly of wood, originally using chalk numbers, hence often being referred to as the slate, and later utilizing plastic numbers attached with Velcro. Almost universally these days, a board known as a backlight board is used and these are a vast

PANAVISION®UK

44501

LONDON 020 8839 7333   LABORATORIES COPY

CONTINUED FROM SHEET No.	SHEET NUMBER	CONTINUED ON SHEET No.

THE SHEET NUMBERS MUST BE QUOTED ON ALL DELIVERY NOTES, INVOICES AND OTHER COMMUNICATIONS RELATING THERETO

PRODUCING COMPANY ....   STUDIOS OR LOCATION ....

PRODUCTION ....   PRODUCTION No. ....

DIRECTOR ....   CAMERAMAN ....   DATE ....

STATE IF COLOUR OR B & W

PICTURE NEGATIVE REPORT

ORDER TO .... LABORATORIES

STOCK AND CODE No.	LABORATORY INSTRUCTIONS RE INVOICING, DELIVERY, ETC.	CAMERA AND NUMBER
EMULSION AND ROLL No.		CAMERA OPERATOR

MAG. No.	LENGTH LOADED	SLATE No.	TAKE No.	COUNTER READING	TAKE LENGTH	'P' for Print B & W	'P' for Print COL'R	LENS F/L & STOP	ESSENTIAL INFORMATION Colour description of scene, filter and/or diffusion used. Day, night or other effects	CAN No.

FOR OFFICE USE ONLY   TOTAL CANS

TOTAL EXPOSED		TOTAL EXPOSED		TOTAL FOOTAGE PREVIOUSLY DRAWN	
SHORT ENDS		HELD OR NOT SENT		FOOTAGE DRAWN TODAY	
WASTE		TOTAL DEVELOPED		PREVIOUSLY EXPOSED	
FOOTAGE LOADED		SIGNED:		EXPOSED TODAY	

Figure 3.4 The laboratory report sheet

Figure 3.5 The clapperboard

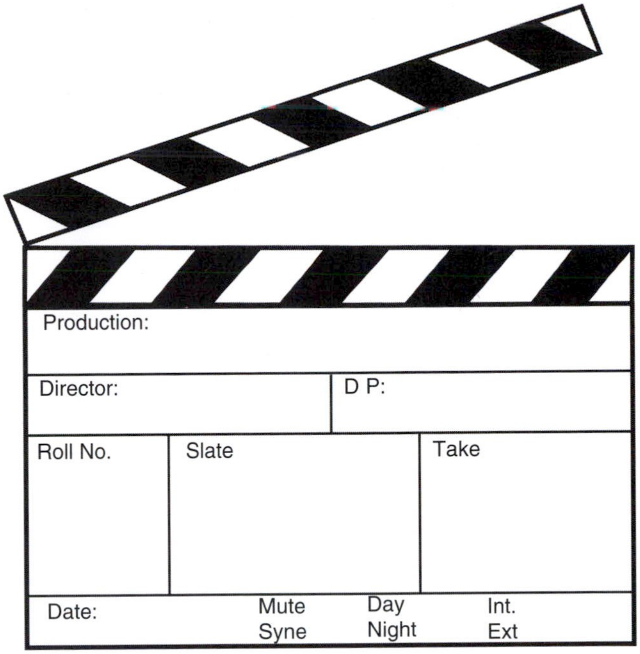

improvement. The stick and an equivalent thickness on the board are still of wooden construction, but the whole of the information section of the board is made from a sheet of opaque, white, acrylic sheet. This has the huge advantage of being capable of illumination from in front or behind. The simple expedient of putting waterproof sellotape on the Production/Director sections, writing on them with pental and then covering them with a second coat of sellotape makes the writing permanent for the duration of the shoot and is still easily removable before the next production. White board wipable markers are used for Roll, Slate and Take. Figure 3.5 shows a typical layout for a backlight board.

Very often, the only way a production judges a clapper loader is by their report sheets and the state of the clapperboard. It is not at all uncommon for a loader to get the chance to work up to focus puller simply on the strength of the immaculate clapperboard the producer has seen every morning at rushes. If there are no hairs in the gate, what else does the producer see of the loader's work?

If there is no trainee on the crew, the loader often brings the camera crew tea and coffee. The DP, the operator and the focus puller can rarely leave the set. Someone has to bring them their tea or they won't get any – so it's the loader or trainee's job.

If you are a loader and you want promotion, be clean and tidy, make up legible, well-written clapperboards and have immaculate report sheets.

It is sometimes the loader's job to negotiate with the production office for expenses and touchy matters like extra money for running a second camera. Great tact is required here, as you can easily fall out with the camera crew and the production office all at the same time. This is clearly not a good plan.

The focus puller (AC1 or 1st AC)

Keeping the main action sharp is the prime responsibility of the focus puller. In addition, they are the one most concerned with the camera itself. It is their task to build the camera each morning and to put it away at the finish of shooting. They must keep it and the lenses scrupulously clean. They must carry out any front-line maintenance on the camera and its associated kit.

Keeping the main action sharp is done, in the main, by using a tape measure, after which the depth of field is calculated using a Kelly calculator, Samcine calculator or depth of field charts (see Chapter 16 for an explanation of this). It takes a great deal of talent and experience to become a good focus puller, and a fine understanding of exactly what the audience will be looking at at any given moment during a scene.

Currently, there is a trend for focus pullers to use infrared range finders. They are very accurate if used with skill. My worry about these devices is that although many of them say they are perfectly safe, we are in a litigious society. Let us suppose the focus puller had put the infrared dot on the forehead of a major star and within a few months that star developed any kind of eye problem – would you want to be in court as the defendant? I would not. Let's stick to the tape – unless we have monumental insurance.

When shooting with lenses with very long focal lengths the focus puller may decide to take an eye focus – that is, focusing the lens through the viewfinder. This is because, with long focus lenses, a very small movement of the focus barrel of the lens may move the plane of focus quite a long way into the set. Before taking an eye focus it is important to know how to set the focus on the eyepiece. First, you rack the focus to a distance which puts the image as out of focus as can possibly be achieved. You then focus the viewfinder on the cross in the middle of the viewfinder. If you now refocus the lens you will have perfect focus.

There is an old trick for obtaining perfect focus that works better in some viewfinders than others. Having obtained what you believe to be a perfectly sharp image, immediately behind the cross in the centre of the viewfinder rock your eye very slightly from side to side. If you are in perfect focus the cross and the image will appear to move together. If you can see any apparent movement between the cross and the image you are not in perfect focus. This is known as parallax focusing, because if you see movement there is a parallax error between the plane of focus of the image and the plane of the cross on the focusing screen. When the image is perfectly formed on the focusing screen, and is therefore sharp, there will be no difference in the position of the image and the cross engraved on the screen and therefore no parallax error.

There are many tricks of the trade and good focus pullers are worth their weight in gold, quite literally, for if the focus puller is first class then the DP may choose to light to a wider aperture and thereby save the production a considerable sum on the lighting budget.

The focus puller is responsible for setting the stop on the lens as directed by the DP.

The focus puller rarely leaves the camera. The operator must be free to go off with the director and the DP to recce the coming set-ups, etc. The loader will bring the focus puller the bits of kit needed to build the camera for the next shot. You could say that, during the shooting day, the camera belongs to the focus puller.

At the end of every printed take the focus puller will check the gate for any hairs or scratches. If all is well, they will then give whoever is on continuity the details of the shot. This will include the focal length of the lens, the focus setting and the stop. On some crews the loader does this, especially if they are keeping very full notes for themselves or the DP; my loader does this for me.

The camera operator

The duties of the operator may seem self-evident, but have you thought of the many different ways that the operator may be asked to interact with the director, the DP, the rest of the crew and often continuity?

It is common in the UK for a director, after giving initial guidance to the DP and usually in the presence of the operator, to leave the DP to their own devices and to work very closely with the operator. In America, most often, the director only talks to the DP; the DP then directs the operator.

Vital to the relationship between the DP, the operator and the director, in the UK way of working, is the ability of the operator to feed back to the DP updates of the director's requirements, which may have happened while the DP was lighting the current set or away pre-lighting another.

When setting camera flags for backlights, etc., the operator must be certain that they are not flagging off light important to the DP's vision of the scene. A continual dialogue between these two most important technicians is imperative. In the UK, the DP or the gaffer sets the flags, in the USA it's the grip's job.

The operator is usually nominated by the DP, but this is a nomination that must always be cleared with the production office. Many directors are as concerned to hire the most appropriate operator as the right DP. It sometimes happens that the director will nominate the operator and ask the DP's approval. As you will appreciate, for a DP to have a regular and admired operator can be an advantage to everyone.

While the operator is responsible for all the camera movements during the shot, they are not responsible for the physical movement of the camera between shots. This falls to the team of focus puller, loader and grip. During a shot the travelling movement of the camera is the responsibility of the grip, working under the direction of the operator.

The Director of Photography

Although I started this book with a more detailed description of the DP's role, I am including here a more general view on the craft in order to see the DP's responsibilities within the overall concept of the camera crew.

The primary responsibility of the DP is to create the mood and feel of the picture with their lighting. Depending on the style of the director, you may be left to decide the look of the film for yourself or, after meetings with the director and, usually, art department, you may then be left to light the set as you see fit. Alternatively, the director may have very firm ideas as to how the film should look and it will be the DP's task to fulfil these wishes. All these different ways of working are just as enjoyable; a little guidance on the set is very fulfilling, but working to a director's wishes and giving what is wanted, and hopefully more, brings much praise and loyalty from the director.

As the senior head of department, the DP is looked to to set an example to the rest of the unit. It is often the personal style of the cinematographer that will get further work just as much as the quality of the photography. Time keeping, crew behaviour, dress and manners all come, at least in part, from the DP and so they set the standard for the professional approach of the crew.

DPs are responsible for all matters pertaining to the photography of the film – lighting, exposure, composition, cleanliness, etc. are all, ultimately, their responsibility. DPs will more often than not nominate the crew – that is, they will have put into the production office a list of first choice and second choice people to be offered the job. If a crew member is nominated by the DP, then the DP is responsible for them and will in all probability have to decide whether they are to be fired if they are not up to the required standard. The upside of this is that DPs usually get the crews they want.

It should be said that it is quite common these days for the DP's contract to include the requirement to provide a 'full negative'. This means that underexposure as a route to providing a certain look is unacceptable to the production. You may find this offensive or restricting, but I am afraid that many producers have had a considerable amount of trouble producing first-class release prints. Though the rushes may look excellent, cinema release prints are usually made from internegatives, as the original negative is far too precious to use for final printing of the large quantity of prints needed by the distributor (see Chapter 8). It is very difficult to make a satisfactory internegative from a thin or underexposed camera negative.

It is not at all uncommon for an appreciable part of the production's budget to come from pre-selling the video rights. A full negative is vital in these circumstances, as the telecine machines used to make the master tape are very intolerant of a thin negative.

I am including all this because cinematographers should get used to producing a correctly exposed negative – bad habits formed early may lead to considerable periods of unemployment later.

The grip or dolly grip

The grip is primarily responsible for the camera dolly and all the movements made by it. They are also responsible for moving the tripod to the next set-up; the focus puller will usually take the camera. Never move a camera while it is still on the tripod. I have seen one fall off in these circumstances – not a pretty sight and very embarrassing.

The grip is responsible for building, or supervising the building of, any construction needed to support the track or boards the dolly is going to run on. The levelling and smoothness of the dolly's working surface is vital to the success of a dolly shot.

Front-line maintenance of the dolly and its kit are down to the grip. Very often, they will have built or had built many special bits to enable

them to fix a camera to almost any object. A good and experienced grip's van is an Aladdin's cave.

The gaffer

The gaffer is the chief electrician and works directly for the DP. Some DPs will set their own flags and barn doors and some won't – it just depends on how they like to work together. Very often, the DP will be closer to his gaffer than any other member of the crew. They are vital to his success.

It is said that one very well known and much respected American DP, when asked by a student what was the single most important thing they could do to improve their photography, replied 'hire the best gaffer you can afford, even if you have to give them part of your fee'. I must say I agree with that advice.

The best boy is simply the gaffer's best boy. On a large crew, the gaffer will plot the cable runs and how to fix and support the lamps – it's the best boy's job to organize the lighting crew and actually move and fix the lamps. On most small units, say three sparks in total, the gaffer acts as his own best boy.

My gaffer and I do most of the tweaking between us, unless it is a big set where I leave it entirely to my gaffer and his best boy. My regular gaffer is so good and understands lighting so well that I will often ask him to light simple set-ups without me there and without a plot. I just have to give him an idea of how I want the artists to look and the mood of the scene, perhaps adding where a main key light should be. On larger set-ups, I give him a floor plan of the set with all the main lamps marked on it; this is then known as the lighting plot, and often he will have to go off with this and put in a very big pre-light without me, as I need to stay with the principal artists.

Crew protocol

On any film set, the camera crew always arrive at least half an hou before the call on the call sheet. The camera will be built and ready o the tripod or dolly before the call time and will be positioned roughl where the first shot of the day is expected. Breakfast is usually take after the camera is prepared. It will not be taken after the call; if yo arrive too late for breakfast, tough, the camera comes first. It is you responsibility to be on time. More technicians lose work through ba timekeeping than anything else, so don't be late – be half an hour earl and get into the habit.

On a feature film, it is traditional for all the other technicians to ca the DP and the director 'Sir'; the DP very often calls the director 'Sir' well, perhaps because in the first few days he can't remember the name and the habit just sticks. You may not approve but you may als get fired if you don't. If 'Sir' has become your habit, then working wi lady directors or DPs can cause embarrassment; wait and see what the seem to prefer. I know one lady director who likes to be called 'Skippe but I wouldn't try that unless you are very, very sure she will like it.

If you show respect to others you are likely to receive it in return film sets are not unlike the rest of life.

Part Two
The Technology

4
The motion picture camera

Man has been beguiled by the movies for over a century now. One reason might be that it takes a disarmingly simple piece of equipment, the motion picture camera, to record images from the most fertile of our imaginations.

In essence, a motion picture camera is a couple of boxes, one with a lens on the front and a mechanism inside capable of dragging a length of film down a specific distance at least 16 times a second, and the other containing a suitable length of film to feed the mechanism with space remaining to take up the film after exposure.

When the pictures from this device are projected by a similar mechanism they give a valid representation of the original scene, with all the movements contained therein correctly displayed in a realistic way.

The persistence of vision

Producing moving images from a length of still pictures relies on what might be considered an aberration in the process of human vision. If an image is flashed upon the retina of the eye the person sees that image, briefly, in its entirety and then, over a short period, the image stays with the person while growing fainter or decaying. If a second image is flashed on the retina, soon enough the person will see the two images as a continuous image without the first flash.

If there is movement in the interval between the flashing of the images, the brain will perceive the difference between the two images as continuous movement providing the time gap between the two images is short enough. If a continuous stream of images is flashed upon the retina in a quick enough succession, then the person will perceive no flashing effects and will perceive the images as a continuous, smooth motion.

The rate of image flashing at which the eye starts to perceive motion is around ten flashes per second, though at this rate a flickering effect will be very noticeable. Only at around 16 or 18 new images per second

Figure 4.1 The decay of an image
on the human retina

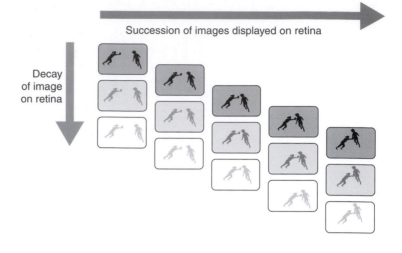

does the movement become truly believable, as continuous motion and the flickering effect reduce to the point where it can be ignored.

Figure 4.1 shows a series of images as they decay, represented by the vertical frames, and the frequency with which the images must be replaced for the observer to believe that they are seeing a smooth, continuous motion, represented by the horizontal frames.

Frame rates

At the turn of the century, a taking frame rate of 16 frames per second (fps) was becoming common practice. At this time, both cameras and projectors were still very much hand cranked and most were geared such that a constant cranking speed of two turns per second resulted in this frame rate, which was very convenient. Those in the industry who were beginning to consider themselves artists would have preferred a higher rate, since this reduced the flicker on the screen, hence the phrase 'going to the flicks'. The film producers and distributors, on the other hand, were seriously opposed to an increase in frame rate, as this would use more film and therefore put up costs. Little has changed.

By 1926, the American Society of Motion Picture Engineers (SMPT, later the SMPTE) Standards and Nomenclature Committee recommended camera cranking speeds as follows:

Regarding camera speed we recommend as a recommended practice: a camera cranking speed of 60 feet per minute (16 fps), with a minimum of 55 feet and a maximum of 65 feet when normal action is desired, in connection with the Society of Motion Picture Engineers recommended practice of 80 feet per minute projection speed (21 fps).

To recommend different taking and projection speeds may now seem ridiculous, but what they were trying to do was to set a standard for a frame rate that was perceived to be correct on viewing. Try turning the sound off on your television and notice how the action suddenly seems to be slower, despite your certain knowledge that it cannot be. It would be uncharitable to think that the theatre owners were keen to reduce the length of the shows so as to pack more audiences in – wouldn't it?

The result of this is that from the turn of the century to the coming of sound, the camera frame rate was set at roughly 16 frames per second. When sound recorded optically on the same film as the picture came in around 1927, the frame rate of 16 fps or 60 feet of film per minute was too slow to make an adequate sound recording using the optical recording techniques available at the time. A faster speed was needed to enable more frequencies to be recorded. By now, it was known that the flicker apparent in a film projected at 16 fps, or thereabouts, started to disappear above a projection rate of 20 fps. At 30 fps it appeared to disappear completely even on the most demanding scenes – these usually being those with pronounced highlights, as flicker is more discernible in the brighter areas of a scene.

In America, the mains electricity has a frequency of 60 cycles per second (cps); therefore, a standard synchronous electric motor there will have a shaft speed of 1440 revolutions per minute. This gives a shaft speed of 24 revolutions per second. The Americans, who after all pioneered the making of the talkies, therefore chose the very convenient frame rate of 24 fps as being almost totally free of any flicker, producing a linear film speed sufficiently high to enable good sound to be recorded next to the picture on the same piece of film and being absurdly simple to drive the projectors at a constant speed from a simple synchronous motor; 24 fps is still today the world standard frame rate for theatrical motion pictures.

For television, matters are slightly different. The television scan rate is inexorably linked to the frequency of the local mains; therefore, in America, where the local mains frequency is 60 cps, the televisions will display a complete picture 30 times per second. To overcome the discrepancy between the theatrical cinema frame rate of 24 fps and the television rate of 30 fps they, effectively, show every fourth frame twice. For high-quality commercials for television in the USA, it is not uncommon to increase the taking rate to 30 fps.

In the UK and other parts of the world, where the mains frequency is 50 cps, this results in a completed frame rate of 25 fps. It is normal to shoot at 25 fps if the film is intended only for television release. Feature films are still shot at 24 fps and, when shown on television, run 4 per cent faster than in the cinema and therefore the overall duration is also reduced by 4 per cent. This makes little difference – remember the SMPE 1926 recommendation of a taking to projection discrepancy of 25 per cent. The only perceivable drawback is a very slight change in the pitch of the sound, which would only be noticeable to someone having perfect pitch. I have only ever known one person comment on this effect and today pitch correction circuitry is available at a very reasonable cost.

The intermittent mechanism

The heart of a film camera, the mechanism that enables it to take a series of still pictures, is known as the intermittent mechanism. To be successful, a film camera must divide the picture-taking cycle, usually evenly, between a period where the film is absolutely still and revealed to the taking lens and a period when the light from the lens must be

Figure 4.2 The 180° revolving shutter

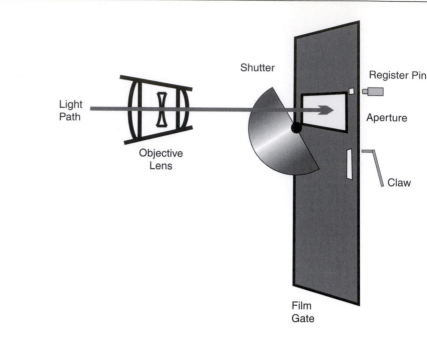

blanked off to enable the film to be pulled down to the next position ready to expose the next frame. To do this, a number of devices are employed:

1   A shutter to blank off the aperture while the mechanism pulls the film through ready for the next frame to be exposed.
2   A channel, or gate, in which to position the film accurately.
3   A device to pull the film down to its next position, usually a 'claw'.
4   Loops of film top and bottom of the film gate to act as reservoirs during the pull-down period.

The shutter

In a film camera the shutter is usually a rotating disc placed immediately in front of the film gate and having a segment removed to allow light to pass to the aperture for exposure while, for the other part of the cycle, the remaining part of the disc rotates to blank off the light during the period in which the film is moving to the next frame to be taken at the same blanking rate as the camera frame rate. Figure 4.2 shows a classic 180° shutter between the taking lens and the aperture in the film gate.

Some cameras use a twin-bladed shutter, often known as a 'butterfly' shutter, as illustrated in Figure 4.3. This is claimed to be better balanced and therefore reduce vibration and, as it has two blades, the shaft speed can be reduced to half that with a 180° shutter and this is said to help reduce camera noise.

The film gate

Behind the shutter will be the film gate, which is made to a very high accuracy in order to keep each frame in exactly the same position,

Figure 4.3 The twin-bladed shutter

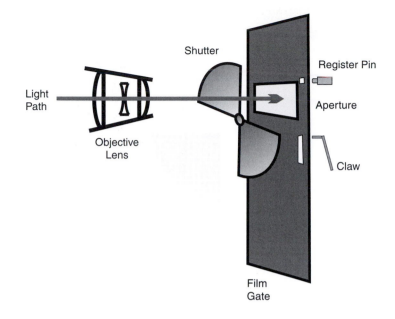

laterally, as its neighbours. The gate is usually several frames long and will have a slot in it to allow the claw to enter the perforations in the film and another to allow a register pin if this is used in the camera's design.

The claw

The most common mechanism for moving the film from one frame to the next is known as a claw, simply because when they were invented they looked like an animal's claw, an arm with a hook or nail on the end. Figure 4.4 shows an early Williamson mahogany-cased, hand-cranked camera, which has recently shot some very good pictures. Despite its age, it graphically shows the classic layout of an intermittent mechanism.

Figure 4.5 shows the current Panavision lightweight camera mechanism, one of the best in the business. Despite being much more sophisticated, it has remarkable similarities to the Williamson – two sprockets top and bottom of the camera box and claw, now much more sophisticated and precise, with the addition of a register pin. In order to improve the vertical alignment, many cameras now provide a register pin or pins that are inserted into perforations adjacent to the aperture just as the claw is retracting and remain there for the duration of the exposure. Figure 4.5 shows Panavision's solution to this challenge. The horizontal bar with the drilled holes right in the middle of the picture is the register pin operating leg; there is a drop bar just behind the gate to locate the actual register pins in the two perforations at the bottom of the frame. In this camera, the claw mechanism is operated by a link mechanism, which can be seen just below the register pin actuating bar.

In many camera mechanisms, one of the complications is that if the gate is straight the claw must have some means of converting the rotary motion of the drive shaft into an absolutely straight movement at the claw tip, as in the Williamson layout. This can lead to inaccuracies,

Figure 4.4 An early Williamson
camera mechanism

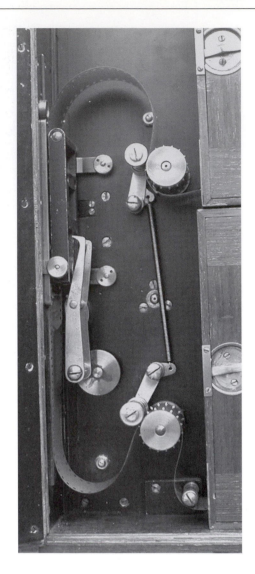

vibration and noise. The Panavision mechanism echoes the earlier Mitchell mechanism in curving the bottom of the gate so that the claw is only required to follow this curved portion of the gate. This design leads to a very vibration-free claw movement of superb accuracy, which is incredibly quiet.

The claw mechanism has to be made to the highest possible tolerances, as the distance each frame is moved must be identical and must be repeated, exactly, every time. When you realize that, during a 10-minute roll of film, the claw will have pulled 16 000 frames of film through the camera, you get some impression of both the precision and durability required of the claw mechanism.

The loop

Between the box holding the reserve and used film, known as the film magazine, and the box containing the camera mechanism and the camera gate will be one or two sprocket wheels with teeth that engage

Figure 4.5 The Panavision
lightweight camera mechanism

with the film's perforations and geared to the claw mechanism, thus ensuring a constant supply of film both to the gate and taking the film away after exposure. As the sprocket will be running continuously and the claw only acts intermittently above and below the gate, the film is allowed to form loops. The loop above the gate forms a reservoir of film ready for the claw to pull it through the gate; this action then enlarges the loop at the bottom of the gate ready for the sprocket to take it away.

The complete cycle of an intermittent movement is shown in Figure 4.6. In film strip A, the frame being exposed is just coming to the end of its full exposure. The shutter is starting to close, the claw is entering the appropriate perforation and the register pin is withdrawing. In film strip B, the shutter is closed, the register pin is fully retracted and the claw is commencing the pull-down. In film strip C, the shutter is still closed, the register pin still withdrawn and the claw is halfway through the pull-down. In film strip D, the shutter is still closed, the register pin still withdrawn but the claw is nearing the end of its travel and starting to slow down. In film strip E, the film has come to rest, the shutter is starting to open, the claw is withdrawing and the register pin is nearly fully in to its perforation. In film strip F, the shutter is fully open, thus starting the exposure, the register pin is fully locked into its perforation, thus holding the frame being exposed absolutely still, and the claw is travelling upwards behind the gate to return to the top of its travel. In film strip G, the shutter is still open, the register pin is still in and the claw has nearly reached its topmost position. In film strip H, the shutter has closed, the register pin has withdrawn and the claw has entered the perforation relating to the next frame and is just starting its pull-down. The cycle is now complete – the mechanism is back to film strip B and will now commence the whole cycle again.

The reflex viewfinder

Early film cameras had viewfinders either by the side or above the taking lens. The viewfinder, therefore, didn't see exactly the same frame

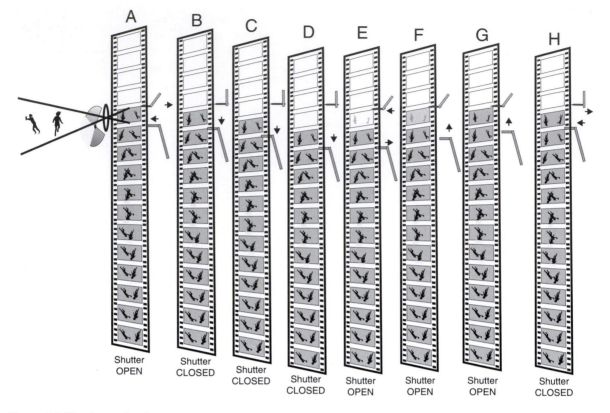

Figure 4.6 The claw and register pin cycle

as the cameras lens. This is known as parallax error, as the optical axis of the taking lens and that of the viewfinder will point in the same direction but will run parallel to each other. This problem was first overcome when a German company, Arnold & Richter, introduced their Arriflex 35 mirror reflex camera to the world at the 1937 Leipzig Fair. This camera totally revolutionized the way film cameras were designed from then on.

The Arriflex did not have its shutter running flat to, and in the same plane as, the film gate but had it angled at 45° to the gate and the aperture. Furthermore, the front surface of the shutter had a mirrored surface, so that when the shutter was closed the light that was blocked from the aperture was now sent off at a right angle. This image was then displayed on a ground glass whose distance from the lens, via the mirrored shutter, was exactly the same as the film aperture. A second fixed mirror, or prism, then sent the image on the ground glass to the viewfinder optics. Thus, the image in the viewfinder was identical to that on the film, as they shared the light from the lens on an alternating basis.

The original Arriflex was organized so that the mirrored shutter sent the light horizontally to the viewfinder. Today, cameras divide between those that send it horizontally and those that have the shutter beneath the lens and send it upwards to the viewfinder. Interestingly, Arriflex have made cameras with both configurations. Figure 4.7 shows the arrangement of a reflex viewfinder where the light is sent upwards.

Figure 4.7 The mirror reflex
viewfinder

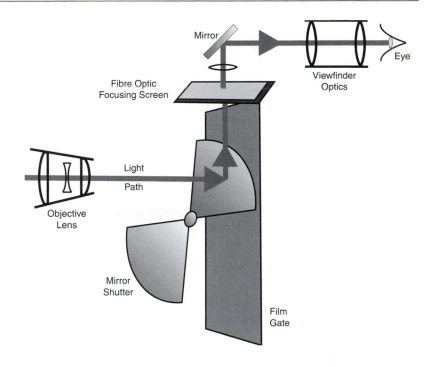

Figure 4.7 The mirror reflex viewfinder

Viewing screens

The ground glass viewing screens of the early reflex cameras have now
been replaced with a slice of an end-on bunch of fibre-optics cut, and
ground flat, to produce a focusing screen. This greatly reduces
vignetting at the edges of the image, is much more critical of exact
focus so that the camera operator can determine the focus more easily, forms an image far brighter than a ground glass and has less brightness fall-off in the corners of the frame.

There is a very reliable way of setting your eyepiece to your natural
vision. Point the camera at an object less than six feet, or two metres,
away, and now rack the lens to infinity – use a lens of at least the
'normal' focal length and focus the viewfinder ocular on the cross in
the middle of the viewfinder, if there isn't a cross focus on the line
around the viewfinder mask. Now refocus on the scene and you will be
able to eye focus perfectly.

The film magazine

In order to be able to change from one roll of film to another at any
time, both the feed roll of film and the take-up roll are housed in a
light-tight container provided with a light trap, through which the film
can exit and re-enter the box – this assembly is known as the film
magazine.

Two configurations of magazine are common today. The first is the
displacement magazine, where both rolls are held in a single chamber,
as shown in Figure 4.8. The displacement magazine takes advantage of

Figure 4.8 The displacement film magazine

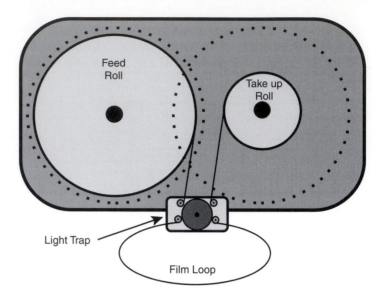

the fact that while the take-up roll is getting larger, as film is exposed, the feed roll is decreasing in diameter. In Figure 4.8, the dotted lines represent where a full feed roll and a full take-up roll would sit in the magazine. Clearly, there is not enough room for both of them. By carefully siting the hubs that will hold the plastic cores the film will come on, the magazine can be laid out so that even if the feed and take-up rolls do get close to each other they will never actually touch.

This has two advantages: firstly, the magazine will be smaller than a design not taking advantage of the displacement effect; secondly, the whole device will be lighter, this being particularly valuable when the camera is to be hand-held or fitted to a steadycam rig.

At the bottom of the magazine illustrated in Figure 4.8 can be seen a light trap. This may consist of either a sprocket or large felt roller in its centre, with four felt rollers, two on the film side and two on the daylight side of the complete trap. By arranging light baffles within and around this arrangement, the designer can ensure that no light from the outside can enter the film chamber even in the brightest sunlight.

If a sprocket is used in the light trap then, when loading the film in the dark, the size of the film loop on the outside of the magazine will have to be carefully set. If the light trap uses only felt rollers, then there is no need to establish an exact loop size when loading the magazine. When this type of magazine is fitted to the camera, having laced the film around the camera's mechanism, either the take-up roll will have to be tensioned by hand or, on some cameras, a lace button is pressed and the magazine feed and take-up motors automatically adjust the spare film, exiting and entering the light trap to exactly the right tension.

An alternative layout is the coaxial magazine. Here the feed and take-up rolls sit side by side, and an arrangement of sprockets and rollers deliver the film to the camera gate in the necessary straight line path. A representation of this can be seen in Figure 4.9.

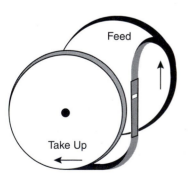

Figure 4.9 The film path of a coaxial magazine

Film camera layout

There are many individual layouts for a film camera, but Figure 4.10 shows the basic principle of most of them. Once the film magazine is fitted to the camera, the loop coming from the camera can be laced through the camera mechanism. It usually has to pass over a sprocket wheel, shown as the dotted circle, and is kept in place by lay-on rollers, shown as the grey circles. Having left the sprocket, the film forms the film feed loop; it then passes through the film gate, with its associated aperture and claw mechanism, and so on to the take-up loop, back over the sprocket, and finally returns to the magazine light trap.

Some cameras employ a quite different layout, where the main sprocket and the back pressure plate of the gate are contained in every magazine. In this instance, the claw mechanism must be in front of the gate. One configuration of this layout is shown in Figure 4.11. During fitting the magazine, shown in the darker grey, slides horizontally towards the camera body, shown in lighter grey. Clearly, the loop

Figure 4.10 Typical layout of a film camera

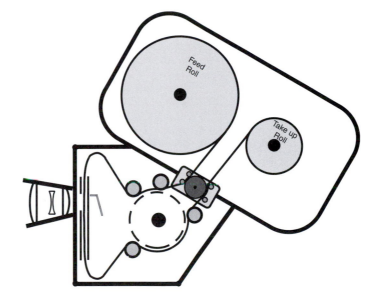

Figure 4.11 The layout of a film camera using clip-on magazines

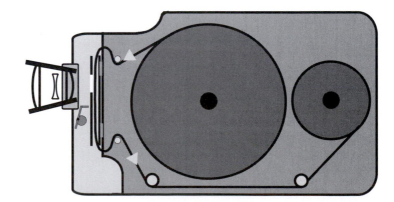

size and its position relative to the gate must be carefully set before the magazine is fitted, and this makes for a slightly more difficult loading procedure in the dark. Many cameramen feel that the advantages of almost instant camera reloads and smaller overall camera configuration more than make up for the slight complication in loading the magazines.

Magazines for this type of layout are often of the displacement type, though some have a configuration of clip-on and coaxial layout, the Arri 16 SR III being one such. The Aaton 35 III takes the concept of displacement one stage further by actually moving the position of the take-up hub during filming, so that the maximum distance between the hubs can be reduced still further, thus making the magazine even smaller and lighter in this very compact and elegant 35 mm camera.

5
Lenses

Artistic decisions

When you come to order a lens set for a picture, you are faced with a number of interesting problems and choices. These relate to:

- Definition or sharpness.
- Speed or maximum aperture.
- Contrast, or how quickly does black become white?
- Do you need prime lenses, a zoom or both?
- What focal lengths do you need? Should you include extreme wide angle or telephoto?

Lenses have developed dramatically over the last 20 years. During this time there have been two areas where lens designers have concentrated their efforts – speed and definition. In doing this, they have developed some amazing lenses but we, as artists, do not always want enormously high definition images nor always need a large maximum aperture.

It is common, especially on feature films these days, to shoot with some kind of diffusion filter on the lens – so why do we assume that the character of the picture will be what we desire when a high definition lens has some of that definition destroyed by a filter? Could we not choose a lens that has the natural characteristic we desire without needing the filter – and would that be an advantage?

Characteristics of lenses

Today, we think of our lenses in very critical technical terms. However, it is as interesting to think of their emotional character. What follows must, of its nature, be broad generalizations and very much my personal opinion:

- German lenses are crisp, analytical and fast. Clinical, even.
- English prime lenses are traditionally warm, emotional, have dark moody shadows and come with a relatively high definition.
- The English Cooke zooms are very gracious in their shadow rendition. I am biased, for if I am going to use a zoom then it is most likely to be a Cooke. The Cooke 18–100 mm T3 zoom for 35 mm is,

in my view, one of the finest lenses ever produced – I shot over 90 per cent of my last picture through one. With 16 mm, the Canon 8–64 mm zoom is also a fine lens that I use a lot.

- American lenses tend to have a high technical specification, are generally reasonably sharp and are physically wonderful to look at.
- Japanese prime lenses have, until recently, mostly been derived from lenses originally computed for still cameras. They have tended to be a little too high in contrast for motion picture work, have unfamiliar maximum apertures and do not come in matched sets. This is changing – the Canon 8–64 mm zoom mentioned earlier was originally computed for video use but has adapted to motion pictures superbly. Indeed, Canon lenses do seem to suit cinematography better than most lenses derived from the stills and video world.
- French lenses are, in the main, a mystery to the English, though they are a little more favoured by American cinematographers. The French 'look' is very attractive and has been going for some time. The desire for a particular feel to the images has influenced both French cameramen and their lens designers. They have been working in sympathy with each other and to each other's advantage.

The other nations' lens designers have also been giving their customers what they want. As a result of this, the knowledgeable cinematographer has a tremendous selection of glassware.

The fundamentals

In order to achieve a higher definition when tested on a lens chart, which usually contains finer and finer black and white lines, the lens designer trades contrast against definition. If you want to resolve black against white, you need a lens with high contrast and very little internal flare; this adds to the measurable definition under these conditions.

If, on the other hand, your main consideration is a long tone range, you might trade off a little contrast and a lower measured definition in order to get a gentler, and perhaps more pleasing, gradation.

Given that the current fashion is for a slightly diffused, 'natural' image, then you might trade off a little speed, contrast and definition for a lens that gave you what you wanted without the need for filtration.

Perceived sharpness with regard to contrast

The eye/brain combination perceives sharpness quite differently from the way we might measure resolution on a lens testing bench. Perception is an impossible thing to measure yet we, as cinematographers, need to get a grasp of how our audience will see our work and need to know if they will consider our pictures to be sharp.

Increasing the contrast of a scene will, most likely, increase the *perceived* sharpness of the scene. That said, it might also reduce the artistic value of the scene or even take it away from the cinematographer's initial concept of the scene as represented in the script. A cinematographer might wish to show a scene with a reasonably high resolution but having a gentle, low-key feel to it. To do this, the cinematographer needs lenses that have a very long tone range and a gentle contrast, but that still appear to be sharp.

Figure 5.1 The relationship
between resolution and contrast

Let us look at some of the sharpness we perceive in a scene as
against the actual resolution of the image. In Figure 5.1, we have two
nearly identical images. Don't study them too carefully, but at a glance
which do you think is the sharper? I would guess you chose the bottom
one. Wrong! All the images for this example were taken on my Nikon
CoolPix camera; the top picture was downloaded at 300 dots per inch
(DPI) and the lower picture at 75 DPI. The difference is the top picture, at the higher resolution, has a much lower contrast than the bottom picture – contrast has fooled you into thinking the resolution is
higher when the contrast is higher.

Figure 5.2 When contrast only
makes a difference

Now look at Figure 5.2. Which do you think is sharper here? I guess
you will again choose the bottom picture. Both pictures were downloaded at 300 DPI, so they both have the same resolution. Again, it is
the higher contrast of the bottom picture that makes it look sharper.

Don't look at Figure 5.3 until you are holding the book at arm's
length and then try and decide which picture is sharper. My guess is
you will think they both look the same. Now bring the book to your
normal reading distance, normally 10 inches or 25 centimetres. If you
look at the top of the gate, you should see a jagged line in the bottom
picture but a true and straight one in the top picture. Both pictures
have exactly the same contrast, but the top picture has a resolution of

Figure 5.3 How viewing distance affects the judgement of resolution

300 DPI and the bottom a resolution of 75 DPI, proving, I hope, that viewing distance is also a critical factor.

The conclusion from all this is that a lens that appears sharp may not be so; it is therefore important that you measure resolution and judge contrast – separately.

Maximum aperture

Let us suppose that you are about to light a picture, during which you do not envisage any scene needing an aperture wider than T3.2. You see the mood of the piece requiring good definition and high contrast

Figure 5.4 The effect of using
different apertures

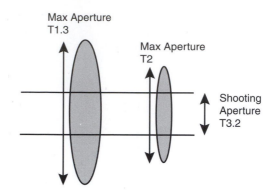

on some scenes, though perhaps not on others. You have decided this
because you want to vary the definition between scenes as part of your
overall strategy for the visual pacing of the film. You will achieve the
variation by the use of filters of different strengths.

You might, say, look to Zeiss Super Speeds as your prime lens set.
They are truly magnificent lenses. But, if you are never going to open
them up beyond T3.2, is this wise? Remember you want maximum
definition in some scenes in order to contrast this with others.

Let us compare a T1.3 lens and a T2 lens both working at an aperture of T3.2. For simplicity, Figure 5.4 shows a single component lens,
but imagine what happens in a compound retrofocal lens containing
many elements – things are much worse.

As you can see, when both lenses are working at an aperture of T3.2
the light has to go through far more glass in the T1.3 lens than in the T2
lens. Now it should be obvious that the more glass the light has to go
through, at any given aperture, the more aberrations are likely to occur.

So, why expect a T1.3 lens to give a finer picture at T3.2 than a lens
with a maximum aperture of T2? There are strong arguments to say
that it won't.

A further disadvantage is that many lenses with maximum apertures of around T1.3 have minimum apertures of only T11, and at T11
they often perform far from their best – imagine how much glass there
must be right in the centre of such a lens. A lens with a maximum aperture of T2, on the other hand, will usually stop down to T16 or even
T22 – quite an advantage with today's high-speed films.

Telephoto lenses

With telephoto lenses all the above remains true, but you have to take
depth of field into account in choosing which lens to use. There is little
point in trying to do a tricky focus pull on, say, a 300 mm lens at T2.8 if
there is any way you can light up to T4 or better. If the shot is going to
be a nightmare at T2.8, you might be better to swap to a higher speed
film just for that one shot – the extra grain hardly ever shows when it
is cut together. So, if you are going to try and avoid shooting at T2.8
with your 300 mm, why order such a fast lens? A 300 mm T4 lens might
very well perform better at T4 than the T2.8 lens stopped down to T4
or it might not, you would need to run a test.

A telephoto lens is not the same as a prime long-focus lens. Telephoto
means the lens has been optically telescoped and is therefore physically

shorter than its stated focal length. This can make the lens very handy, but does put more glass between the subject and the film plane. A true long-focus lens usually has few elements and is thus optically very pure but has, by its very nature, to be physically at least as long as its prescribed focal length.

As an example, I own a 500 mm prime long-focal-length lens of maximum aperture T5.7, which gives most beautiful pictures, is not too heavy but, with its lens hood, is around 750 mm long. Compare this with a Canon 300/600 mm telephoto lens, which in its 600 mm configuration has a maximum aperture of T4 and is less than 400 mm long. The 'look' on film of the two lenses could not be more different – for drama or feature work I choose my prime 500 mm every time, but a wildlife cinematographer would almost certainly make the opposite choice.

Wide-angle lenses

Wide-angle lenses have a different problem. Imagine looking down the empty lens port of a 35 mm camera and think of a point 18 mm in front of the film plane. You will see that this space is occupied by the mirror shutter when it is in the closed position. How then do we regularly use a lens of 18 mm focal length, let alone shorter? It is achieved by using a retrofocal design. Retrofocal means that the lens contains elements in addition to those forming the 18 mm prime lens, whose sole job is to refocus the rays further away from the back element so that the lens will produce a sharp image at the film plane despite being perhaps, physically, 50 mm or so away. This is one reason why the wide-angle lenses are often the most expensive of a set, as they contain a lot of very sophisticated glass. One of the problems in designing wide lenses is that they are very prone to distortion, usually barrelling.

Zooms

Zoom lenses, by their very design, have far more elements within them than prime lenses and therefore come with all the same problems, plus a few more. Figure 5.5 shows the internal construction of a Cooke 18–100 mm zoom.

Many zooms change the image size when the focus is changed. They may vignette at certain focal lengths, and I have even known one have a colour shift at one end on the zoom range. The problems are minimized by the designers keeping to sensible maximum apertures and not trying to offer too long a zoom range.

Most high-quality 35 mm zooms are around T3 and 16 mm zooms around T2.5. While the 16 mm Zeiss T2 10–100 mm, when first introduced, seemed like a miracle, in fact it was, in my opinion, not as good as its predecessor the T3 10–100 mm in some respects, especially with regard to image shift, vignetting and, at around 16 mm, definition. Most of these problems were ironed out with the introduction of the Mark 2, but this necessitated the use of a much larger front element cluster, and subsequently having to use a different, larger and more expensive matte box.

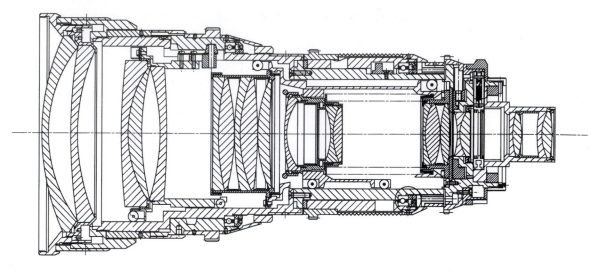

Cooke Lenses 'Classic' 18–100 mm T3 Zoom lens

Figure 5.5 The Cooke zoom

The Cooke 9–50 mm, 10.4–52 mm for Super 16, and the Canon 8–64 mm limit their maximum aperture to T2.5 or T2.8 for the Cooke and T2.4 for the Canon. These sensible apertures and shorter zoom ranges have enabled the designers to produce lenses with virtually no image shift, very high definition and no discernible distortions or vignetting. The same applies to the 35 mm Cooke 18–100 T3 lens of which, as you will have gathered, I am a huge fan.

I realize many cinematographers might disagree, but it really is almost impossible to tell, subjectively, the difference between images shot on any of these zooms and most prime lenses. You might be able to tell when testing but, I submit, it is virtually impossible once the shots have been cut into a narrative scene. Zoom lens design has come a long way since they were first introduced. If you are going to use any kind of filtration then, by balancing its strength, any difference really is impossible to see.

Interestingly, Canon also make an 11.5–138 mm T2.5 zoom for Super 16 mm, which is also a fine lens with just one drawback – there is a noticeable image size change on focusing.

Conclusions

You must be very careful and aware when you choose your lens set. Lenses that, on paper, seem to have a high specification may not perform as well as some others given the way you are going to use them. The character of the lens, under the circumstances you are going to use it, often means more to the cinematographer than the technical specifications of the lens, such as the minimum aperture, which may never be used.

Most importantly, remember that your audience has come to be entertained and will probably never know what lens you used, nor will they care – all they are interested in is that you stir their emotions.

Modern lens designs

Panavision Primo

A few years ago, Panavision introduced a new range of prime lenses called Primos. These were a very successful attempt to offer the cinematographer a new set of lenses that would have, as near as was attainable, totally matching characteristics across the whole range of focal lengths – at this they very much succeeded.

Since the first edition of this book, I have had considerably more experience with Panavision lenses and have had to reconsider my views on them, very much upwards. They appear to have what I can only describe as a clarity, not a very technical term but the one that seems most appropriate. The images they produce are remarkably true to the way my eye sees the set before me and they are superbly sharp, which extends the possibilities of the use of filtration. Their accurate colour correction and consistency from lens to lens makes a DP's life very satisfying when shooting with Primos. Though it's not strictly applicable to the film world, I feel I would like to comment on a couple of Panavision Digital Primos. In the last two years I have had the luck to shoot quite a few projects using the Panavision High Definition cameras and have frequently used the matched pair of 4.5:1 zooms. The wider zoom has a range of 6–27 mm at T1.8 and the longer one a range of 25–112 mm at T1.9. The pictures I have shot using these two lenses on both Panavision's 900 and 750 series cameras have impressed me beyond measure – they are probably the finest lenses I have ever had the pleasure to use.

It would be fascinating to try these Digital Primos reconfigured for Super 16.

Once Panavision had embarked on designing the Primos, all the lenses were calculated to match very closely on many parameters. These included colour rendition, maximum aperture (T1.9), outer barrel configuration and, a great feature of this range of lenses, the optimum definition that is maintained at the maximum aperture.

All the Panavision Primo lenses have the exceptional 'user friendliness' well known and much loved of all Panavision equipment. This, in particular, makes them very popular with all members of the film crew.

Zeiss

Zeiss were one of the earliest lens manufacturers to gain worldwide recognition long before man was able to capture a moving image. They continue to keep a very fine reputation today, having been one of the first manufacturers to produce very high speed lenses, with all the other parameters still of the highest quality.

The Zeiss Distagons, when first introduced, virtually revolutionized shooting 16 mm film overnight. I remember filming in a French restaurant at night with no additional lighting whatsoever. A man passing our unit table mumbled 'It will never come out' with a Gallic shrug and moved on. I wrote on the back of my business card, 'Zeiss Distagon T1.3' and asked a waiter to take it over to his table. Moments later he was by my side holding one of my early Distagons with what can only be described as reverence. Such was the impact of this new and wonderful lens set.

The company's zoom lenses for 16 mm photography are of high quality and have now gone through several generations. I have a particular affection for the original 10–100 mm T3 or T3.1 lens. If you can find one in good condition it is still a very usable lens much, and wisely, favoured by many film schools.

Zeiss now produce high-speed lenses for both 16 mm and 35 mm photography, and they are all of the highest quality with some very interesting variants, including lenses that can be used for normal photography but will focus extraordinarily close.

Cooke lenses (S4 range)

Soon after the introduction of Panavision's Primo lenses, which, of course, you could only hire if you were getting your camera equipment from Panavision, a number of independent camera rental houses realized that they were slightly wrong-footed as they had nothing to offer which might compete with the Primos. The Zeiss super speeds were good but, by comparison, an older generation of computation. So they got together and started asking around as to who might produce something to give them an interesting range to market.

Cooke Lenses had already embarked on the early work of a new range of prime lenses. Here was a wonderful opportunity. Cooke Lenses had, for a couple of generations, been revered for very fine lenses with a certain 'look'. This look is hard to describe and impossible to define in any technical or scientific way. It is an emotional thing: words like romantic, gentle, deep shadows, kind to the artists all come to mind. Nevertheless, Cooke lenses have always had very good definition.

Cooke have, over the years prior to the introduction of the S4 range, produced three important series of prime lenses. The Series 1 range were innovative in their time but now hopelessly out of date. Their Series 2 are famed worldwide. Perceived wisdom, which I agree with, says that a set of Series 2 lenses, with the 18 mm replaced by a Series 3 lens that is superior to the Series 2, may well have been the ultimate set of prime lenses of that era. I have shot two pictures with exactly this set (admittedly they had all been recoated and set in new housings by Century Precision Optics) and received much praise for the results. As a cinematographer, what else does one choose a set of lenses for? Both pictures were, of course, period pieces, where the lenses helped me create the feeling of the times.

Having now tried the Cooke S4 range, I am very impressed. Somehow they have produced an utterly modern set of lenses but have retained the 'Cooke look'.

Cooke have also brought the range very much up to date as regards the mechanical engineering. Having taken note of a modern focus puller's needs, they have completely dispensed with the conventional scroll or screw-thread method of racking the lens in and out to focus it and, borrowing design thoughts from their zoom lenses, used cams and cam followers to give a much more linear feel to the focusing scale, together with greater smoothness. This has enabled them to engrave a very user-friendly focus scale, giving focus pullers much greater control over their craft.

For many cinematographers a huge advantage of the Cooke S4 primes is that they match to extraordinary close tolerances the colour rendition and feel of the Cooke zooms. They are also all optimized to work at their common maximum aperture of T2.

Choice

So which range of lenses should you choose? It doesn't really matter – Ziess, Primos and Cooke S4s are all absolutely superb. What is important is that you read the script first, decide on the look you want and then choose the lens set that suits you best. Today's cinematographers are extraordinarily lucky to have a choice of at least three great sets of lenses.

Lens distortion and aberrations

The three most common forms of optical distortion that occur in lenses are known as pincushion distortion, barrelling and chromatic aberration.

Prime lenses very rarely show any discernible distortion. The exception might be extreme wide-angle lenses, some of which show a slight tendency to barrel.

The finest zoom lenses will show no discernible distortion even at the widest end of their range. Unfortunately, many current zoom lenses, mainly those intended for or derived from those originally intended for video cameras, still demonstrate considerable distortion. Again, the most common or exaggerated distortion is barrelling at the wider end of the zoom's focal range. Because the market for video zooms asks for very high zoom ratios coupled with wide maximum apertures, the manufacturers cannot meet all the parameters of a perfect lens at prices the market will bear.

The manufacturers do their best but, as in all things, you get what you pay for and if you are asking for two of the lenses' attributes to be long zoom range and wide aperture, then almost certainly other parameters of the design will suffer. In this case, the choice usually tends towards a design where a noticeable amount of barrelling occurs at the wide end and very noticeable image size change shows strongly when the focus is changed.

In many applications barrelling and image shifts are not important drawbacks, since the kind of images the lenses will be used to record mask the faults. For news and sport, where the camera is rarely absolutely still, any image shift when focusing will not be noticeable. Slight barrelling will only show where there are vertical lines in the scene near the edge of the frame and, again, this does not occur often in these applications.

The effect of distortion

Figure 5.6 shows a series of shapes in their perfect form. There is a square containing a circle that itself contains another square. Were we to photograph this shape using a lens that suffered from pincushion distortion, then the resultant image would look very much like Figure 5.7, not at all acceptable.

If the same Figure 5.6 was photographed using a lens suffering from barrelling, then the image created would appear as shown in Figure 5.8, again unacceptable.

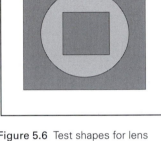

Figure 5.6 Test shapes for lens distortion

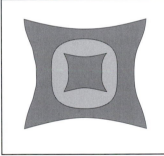

Figure 5.7 Pincushion distortion

Figure 5.8 Barrel distortion

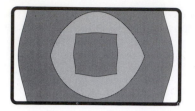

Figure 5.9 Cropped barrel distortion

If either of these distortions are present in the lens in use, the degree of distortion can be measured, but more important is the perceived degree of distortion. You have to look through the viewfinder and decide if you can tolerate the effect you see.

The perceived level of distortion is usually a little less than one might expect, as we are nearly always recording at the film plane a rectangular image taken from the centre of the circular image formed by the lens. Figure 5.9 shows exactly the same drawing as Figure 5.8, but cut down to a 16 × 9 image format.

Although the distortion still looks unacceptable, it now only appears at its worst at the sides of the frame; the overall effect is less to the eye than in Figure 5.8. If you suspect a lens of barrelling then frame a vertical line, say the side of a building, at the edge of the frame and make your own judgement.

Chromatic aberration

Chromatic aberration is the most commonly found aberration in older lenses. It is rarely found in modern lenses, though one occasionally finds it in lenses of long focal length. It is worth understanding, as it displays very clearly one of the major problems lens designers have to overcome; indeed, the correction of chromatic aberration was the first major optical breakthrough in the early days of photography.

Chromatic aberration occurs because light with different wavelengths, or colours, will be diffracted, or bent, by a different amount after having passed through the air/glass, glass/air path as the light travels through a lens.

Figure 5.10 shows, in an exaggerated form, the effect of light passing through a simple lens. The most deviated wavelengths are ultraviolet, shown as UV in the diagram. The least deviated, and therefore those coming to a point of focus furthest from the lens, are the infrared rays, shown as IR in the diagram. In between, at focus points progressively further away from the lens, are blue, green and red.

This effect of focusing the rays of differing colours at different distances from the lens occurs in all simple, single lenses. It has long been a well-known phenomenon: Sir Isaac Newton believed that it was such an intractable problem that he concentrated on reflecting or mirror optics for his telescopes, where the problem does not occur as the light rays never pass through anything but air, thus obviating the problem.

Figure 5.10 Chromatic aberration

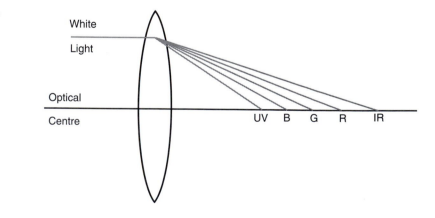

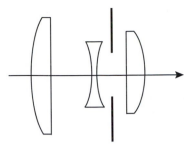

Figure 5.11 The Cooke triplet

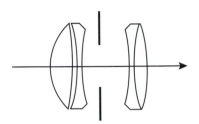

Figure 5.12 The Zeiss Tessar

As glasses of many more densities became available and the value of constructing more complicated lens groups was understood, it became increasingly possible to arrange for more and more wavelengths of light to focus at the same point after passing through the whole of the lens. This was achieved by combining both positive and negative lenses in groups, so that the failings of the individual elements combined to cancel each other out, thus leaving the complete lens aberration-free.

The first lenses that successfully corrected for the three colours of the visible spectrum to converge at the same point of focus were known as triplets, as they were constructed from three single elements having differing curvatures and made from glasses of different densities. Figure 5.11 shows one of the early, successful triplets, from the firm of Cooke, Taylor, Taylor & Hobson, the company now known as Cooke Lenses.

Further developments brought the Zeiss Tessar, as shown in Figure 5.12, where the rear lens of a basic triplet design has two simple lenses cemented together for the rear element, thus enabling the optical designer greater freedom of design.

Lenses have come a long way since the discovery of the basic triplet. For example, the current Cooke S4 25 mm lens – the lens elements here are in double figures and the mechanics of focusing are now much more sophisticated than a simple screw thread. Lenses such as this have eliminated all apparent distortions and aberrations, come in perfectly matched sets and can be utterly relied upon.

6
Film stock

What is film?

Rolls of film are always known as film stock. You will hear unexposed film referred to as raw stock. Once it is exposed, but not yet processed, it becomes known as the rushes. Once exposed and processed, it is the master negative. Confusingly, the print or tape sent back to production by the laboratory the morning after processing is also known as the rushes. In America, these rushes are known as the dailies, which removes the confusion.

Today's colour film stocks are fairly complicated affairs, consisting of a support medium, known as the base, which is coated on one side with as many as nine layers of light-sensitive emulsions. In addition, there are several other layers such as the yellow filter layer. All of these layers are collectively known as the emulsion. The top layer of the emulsion is known as the supercoat, whose purpose is both to protect the film from mechanical damage and to lubricate it through the camera gate. On the reverse side of the base, there is a removable coating called the rem-jet backing. This is black and eliminates halation – haloes around bright points of light. It is anti-static and also lubricated.

The history of the negative/positive photographic process

The knowledge of photosensitive salts was noted by Albertus Magnus as long ago as the thirteenth century. The basis of obtaining an image using these salts was much worked upon but not made practical in the sense we know photography today until the mid-nineteenth century. In 1819, Sir John Herschel, the British scientist, discovered sodium hyposulphate and its ability to dissolve silver chloride. It was not until 1839, 20 years later, that he told his friend William Henry Fox Talbot of the discovery. By this time, Fox Talbot had developed a method of obtaining an image on photosensitive paper using a silver halide as the reactive chemical. The image was a negative one, but he had not found a method of making it permanent, or fixing it. Sodium hyposulphate dissolved out the still sensitive silver halide crystals, leaving stable metallic silver as the image.

It was not until 31 January 1839 that Fox Talbot was able to present a paper to the Royal Society in London showing he could make 'photogenic drawings' or shadows of real objects. By the end of September 1840, Fox Talbot had discovered the theory of the latent image and found a method of developing it and stabilizing it, or fixing it, to an acceptable degree of permanence using Herschel's sodium hyposulphate. This technique he called the Calotype and this was the originator of today's negative/positive photographic process. At this stage, though, both the negative and the positive had to be made on paper soaked in the light-sensitive solution.

In the *British Journal of Photography* of 18 September 1871, an English doctor, Richard L. Maddox, announced his method of spreading a warm solution of gelatine onto glass plates, the gelatine being mixed with cadmium bromide and silver nitrate. Thus, a further step towards modern photography was taken, for now a light-sensitive emulsion could be coated on an independent support material.

By around 1883, further developments in emulsion chemistry had given the world an efficient dry photographic plate, made of glass, which could be prepared long in advance of the need to use it, could be kept for a considerable time after exposure and before development, and required less than a second's exposure in daylight.

By 1889, George Eastman was using a thin film of the plastic celluloid as a base material for the film for his latest amateur still camera and it was the introduction of this support medium, or base, that produced the last factor needed for a film that could be used practically by the inventors of motion picture equipment.

The early film bases were made of nitrocellulose. This produced a very transparent and flexible support. Unfortunately, the material is also highly inflammable and somewhat dimensionally unstable. By 1920, a 'safety' base using cellulose acetate became available that is more stable, slow to ignite and burned at the same rate as paper. It is the instability of the nitrate base that is the main reason for the poor survival of early films. However, nitrate base continued to be used up to the 1950s, when it was phased out.

From this potted history it is reasonable to say that four crucial elements had to be present before a film stock capable of supporting a moving image was available. They were:

1   The discovery of the latent image and how to develop it.
2   The application of a fixer to that developed image to give it permanence.
3   The knowledge of how to incorporate the sensitive chemical in a supporting medium, gelatine, so that it could easily be coated on an independent base.
4   The introduction of a flexible support for the image, celluloid, so that the film could run through an intermittent mechanism.

The basic photographic process

In order to consider the basic photographic process, let us look at a simple black and white film whose physical construction will be much as shown in Figure 6.1.

Figure 6.1 A section through
a black and white emulsion

Basic Black & White Film

Supercoat

Light sensitive emulsion

Adhesive
Layer

Film Base

The emulsion is the light-sensitive layer of the film. It is made up of small crystals of sensitive material evenly distributed in a support medium. The light-sensitive medium is silver halide, derived from pure silver, and the support medium is gelatine, which is made from animal skins and bones.

The gelatine support medium has a number of very useful properties. It is more or less transparent and therefore will let light through to all the sensitive crystals at whatever depth they are embedded in its thickness. It is easily permeated by water, so the various chemicals that are needed to act upon the crystals during processing can reach their target. It is also reasonably easy to produce in a very pure form.

We have seen how various researchers contributed to the discovery of the negative/positive photographic process, but now we must understand something of how it works. I am sure you will have heard of a photographic emulsion as being made up of grains and, indeed, we often refer to the visual texture of a photographic image as being either grainy or, perhaps, having fine grain. The chemical construction of a photographic emulsion starts with a single atom of silver halide; these atoms are then grouped together in varying numbers, some forming small clusters made up of few atoms and some forming large clusters containing many atoms. A typical emulsion will have many sizes of clusters, from really quite large to very small. All of these clusters, whatever their size, are known as the grains in the film.

If part of the photographic image is made up of many small grains, then it might be referred to as being fine grain. This means that there are so many small grains packed so close together that in the final image the human eye will find it very hard to discern one grain from another and the picture, over that area, will look as if it has a continuous smooth tone. If another part of the image is made up of a few large grains, each probably spaced some distance apart, then the eye might be just able to discern the pattern of the grains, and then it will not look very like a continuous tone and we would therefore describe it as grainy.

But how does all this come about? If you look at Figure 6.2 you will see a representation of the layout of different sized grains embedded in the emulsion before any exposure has taken place. To make the following explanation easier, there are only four different sizes of grain shown in the illustration; in reality, there would be a huge number of

Figure 6.2 The grain field

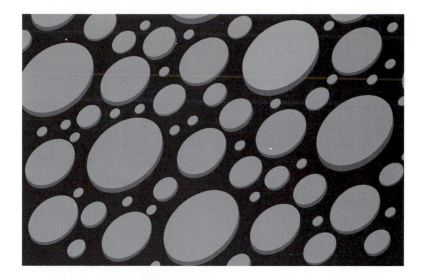

Figure 6.3 Photons hitting
grains

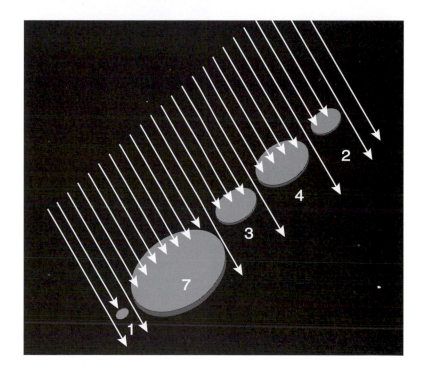

different sizes of grains. For the propose of understanding more
clearly, let us consider one grain of each of the four sizes in our example being hit by an even area of light. Light is made up of particles of
energy we refer to as photons, so if you look at Figure 6.3 you will see
our four different sized grains being attacked by an even array of photons, each represented by an arrow. Because the photons are evenly
spaced and the grains are of differing sizes, the number of photons to
hit each grain will differ.

What will happen next is a chemical reaction. We have seen that
below the grain size there is a molecular structure. Let us suppose, for

Figure 6.4 The result of
exposure

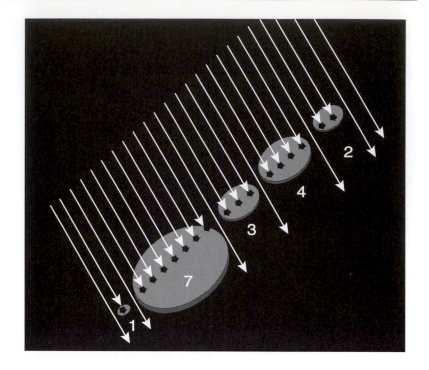

the sake of argument, that every photon strikes an atom of the silver halide. If this is the case, then every photon will cause an atom of silver halide to convert to an atom of metallic silver, as in Figure 6.4. This is the first part of the photographic process. The emulsion will now consist of a number of silver halide atoms and a number of metallic silver atoms. Clearly, we could not see this image as our eyes would need light for that to happen and that would immediately expose every atom in the emulsion. This is, in effect, an image waiting to be made visible and we therefore refer to it as a latent image, the Concise Oxford English Dictionary describing latent as 'Hidden, concealed; existing but not developed or manifest' – exactly the situation our metallic silver image finds itself in.

In order to make the image usable, again in total darkness, we immerse the film in a liquid known as the developer. What happens next is only slightly short of miraculous. The developer is very selective, for if it is applied for the right amount of time, in the correct strength and at the right temperature, it will search out grains containing four or more atoms of metallic silver within them and turn all the atoms to metallic silver, not just those atoms of metallic silver but *every atom of silver halide within that grain as well*. Grains, however big or small, that have three or less grains of metallic silver will be totally unaffected, *not even those atoms that have been turned to metallic silver will become black*. The effect of this is shown in Figure 6.5. There is a danger here, because if silver halide is left exposed to light for a very long time it will eventually turn black without the application of a developer; the developer simply speeds up the process in a carefully controlled manner. Therefore, if we now brought our film out into the light in order to view the image we might see it for a fleeting moment, after which the whole film would turn black before our eyes.

Figure 6.5 After
development

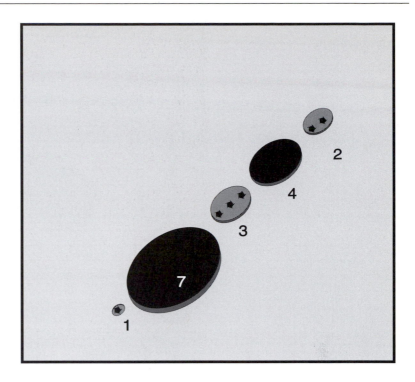

Still in total darkness, and after exactly the right amount of development time, we plunge our film into an acid stop bath. As its name suggests, this immediately stops the process of development but still leaves the image vulnerable to more light. After the acid stop bath, there remain active silver halide grains in the film so, still in complete darkness, the film must now go into a fix bath, which turns the remaining silver halide into substance (complex sodium argentothiosulphates) that can then be washed out of the emulsion without affecting the metallic silver. This chemical, the fixer, is the sodium hyposulphate discovered by Sir John Herschel in 1839, referred to earlier in this chapter. You will occasionally hear the fixer referred to as 'hypo', a name derived from the chemical name of its primary component. So, if the fixer dissolves out of the photographic emulsion all the undeveloped grains but leaves all the developed grains completely unaffected, then our little microcosm of the film will look like Figure 6.6 and will, at last, be safe to bring into the light. The application of all the above liquid chemicals to the emulsion is referred to as processing that emulsion. If you compare Figures 6.2 and 6.7 you will see the effect of processing on the whole grain field.

Now the number of photons in the above example might be considered a medium exposure. Were we to consider a higher exposure, which would be like that found in a much brighter part of the overall scene, then the same four grains we used in the above example would be attacked by a photon array much like that shown in the left of Figure 6.8, but after processing all but one of the grains will be black, as only the smallest grain failed to have four atoms of silver halide turned to metallic silver. In Figure 6.9 we see the reverse, where a dark part of the scene is recorded, and as there are far fewer photons only the largest grain is fortunate enough to have the requisite four atoms

Figure 6.6 After fixation

Figure 6.7 Grain field after processing

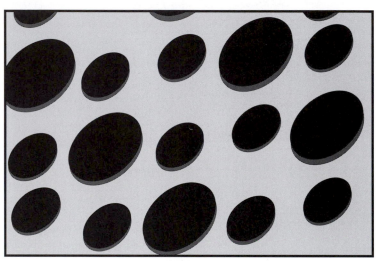

turned from silver halide into metallic silver, resulting, after processing, in only a single grain turning to black.

If the film is to remain in perfect condition for many years it must now be washed for a considerable time, as all the unwanted chemicals must be completely removed and the gelatine emulsion left with only metallic silver to form the image.

Therefore, the image formed by this process will have dark areas where much light fell upon the film and light areas where little light arrived and, fortunately for our purpose, all the shades of grey in between. It will therefore be the reverse brightness of the original scene, and this we call a negative image.

In order to obtain an image that represents the original scene, the negative must be printed on to another piece of film, just as Fox Talbot's process announced in 1839. This new film will produce an image with the reverse densities of the negative and will return to the values corresponding to the original scene. This new film is called the positive and must be processed in exactly the same way as the camera negative.

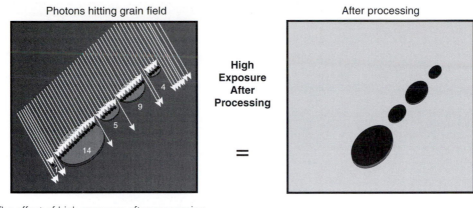

Figure 6.8 The effect of high exposure after processing

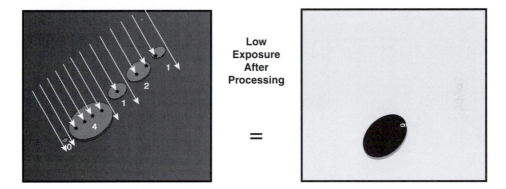

Figure 6.9 The effect of low exposure after processing

Colour negative film

There is no such thing as a single colour photographic emulsion. At its simplest, a modern colour negative film is made up from three black and white emulsions so arranged that each single layer records the image of one of the primary colours that make up white light, i.e. red, green and blue.

If you refer to Figure 6.10, you will see how the layers of coatings on the film base are arranged in order to record a colour image in what is known as an integral tripack colour emulsion. Under the supercoat is the first emulsion. It is relatively easy to make a black and white emulsion that is only sensitive to blue light, so this is used as the uppermost emulsion layer. Underneath this coating is an optical filter layer coloured yellow. A yellow filter will let green and red light through, but not blue. Again, it is possible to make a black and white emulsion that is only sensitive to green and blue light, but all the blue light has now been filtered out, so this layer will only be struck by the green and red light passed by the yellow filter. It will, therefore, only record the green part of the image. The bottom emulsion layer is sensitive to red and blue, but not to green, so this layer can only respond to red as blue has been filtered out.

Figure 6.10 A section
through an integral tripack
colour film

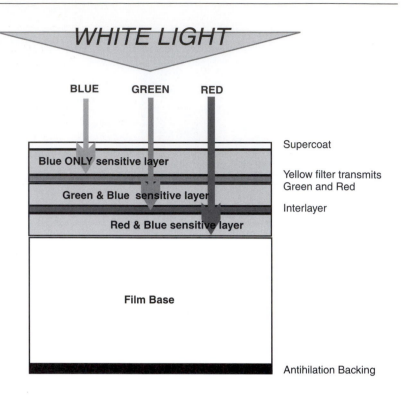

If an exposed film of this type is simply immersed in the standard black and white developer/fixer process, all you will get is three black and white images. Therefore, a clever bit of chemistry is incorporated in each of the three emulsions. The chemicals used are known as colour couplers. Each individual layer has embedded in it a different colour coupler whose job is, at a molecular level, to form a dye of the colour complementary to the colour of the light that exposed the layer. What is more, this dye is formed only where silver is formed by the developer.

As this is a negative film intended for printing, each layer of emulsion must end up dyed the complementary colour to the original scene. Therefore:

- The blue-sensitive layer forms yellow dye.
- The green-sensitive layer forms magenta dye.
- The red-sensitive layer forms cyan dye.

Early colour film was capable of recording roughly seven stops of tonal range or a brightness range of 128:1. Modern film stocks have now been introduced with a tonal range of around 10 stops or a brightness range of over 1000:1.

This has been made possible by the development of super-thin emulsion layers and the concept of coating two or three emulsions to make up each colour layer. Figure 6.11 shows the basic layout of such a film. The trick is to coat layers of emulsion with different sensitivities, e.g. a highly sensitive emulsion, a medium sensitivity emulsion and a slow emulsion, together as a triple layer for each colour. By carefully overlapping the tonal range of each individual emulsion, the film can

Figure 6.11 A section through a modern colour film

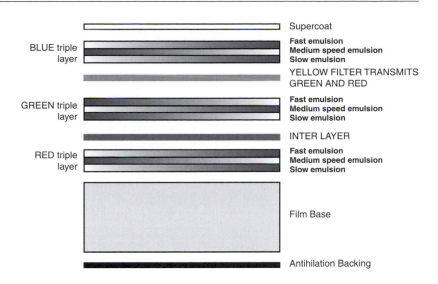

Supercoat

BLUE triple layer
Fast emulsion
Medium speed emulsion
Slow emulsion

YELLOW FILTER TRANSMITS GREEN AND RED

GREEN triple layer
Fast emulsion
Medium speed emulsion
Slow emulsion

INTER LAYER

RED triple layer
Fast emulsion
Medium speed emulsion
Slow emulsion

Film Base

Antihilation Backing

record a tonal range far greater than that of a film having just a single emulsion and with a considerable improvement in image quality.

Grain and graininess

Grain is the texture we see in a print that appears as a texture not associated with the original scene. It becomes apparent when, for various reasons, we can begin to perceive the distribution of the developed metallic silver particles and we can perceive them long before we can actually see any particles. Furthermore, because the print stock is of exceptionally fine grain, and consequently has a very slow speed, the perceived grain comes from the structure of the negative emulsion, not the positive emulsion.

It is thought that a larger crystal of silver halide is more sensitive to light mainly because its surface area is greater and therefore has a better chance of catching a light ray and being exposed. It follows that a film emulsion with a preponderance of large grains will therefore be more sensitive. A fast, highly sensitive film emulsion will normally appear grainy. Conversely, a fine-grained film emulsion has a high resolution and poor sensitivity. At this point it must be said that recent developments in emulsion technology have made the perceivable differences between film stocks of differing speeds much less noticeable than they were even a few years ago.

It is worth considering at this point the difference between resolution and perceived sharpness as it relates to the film emulsion. Resolution is defined as the ability of the emulsion to record very narrow bands of black and white lines and is measured, therefore, as the maximum number of lines per millimetre that can be recorded on the emulsion's surface. Acutance, or what actually looks sharp to the eye, is the ability to record the edge sharpness of an image. Difference in grain size and the contrast of the image will change the relationship of the apparent definition and acutance of a given film stock, and must always be carefully balanced by the emulsion designer. Resolution, acutance and apparent sharpness do not, therefore, always go hand in hand.

When does grain become unacceptable?

Grain will show up first in two areas of the final image and in both cases it derives from the metallic silver image created on the negative.

Firstly, it will appear in the continuous mid-tones. Think of a continuous blue summer sky photographed using a polarizing filter. Here we have a continuous, unrelieved density on the print very closely approximating a tone close to the middle of the tonal range the film can record. If there is the slightest grain or microscopic variation in density, then our audience, whether they be photographically educated or not, will immediately know that this effect is totally unreal, i.e. it doesn't happen in nature. For this reason their eye will immediately be drawn to this unnatural phenomenon. Secondly, grain becomes very noticeable if it is too apparent in the shadowed part of the final image. This is a photographic problem since, on the negative, where dark areas are represented by pale areas, there are few exposed silver particles. This continuous tone is one with only a few exposed grains scattered about. Again, we have a situation where the audience's awareness demands that black is black and not something approximating it with a few bits of information, the silver crystals, 'boiling' in the darkness.

The solution to the mid-tone problem is to choose a film stock with a fine enough grain for the problem never to be apparent to the audience. The solution to the second problem, grain noticeable in the shadows, is to give the shadows just a little exposure above the bottom threshold of the film's recording ability, so that there are just enough grains in that area of the negative to deceive the audience's eye into failing to see the image of the silver crystals. To discover how to do this, refer to Chapter 12.

Perforations

Film stock is manufactured in what are known as parent rolls, usually 6000 feet long and around a metre and a half wide. The parent roll therefore needs to be cut, or slit, into the required width of 16, 35, 65 or 70 mm. It is usual to slit the whole parent roll into just one film width. Having slit the parent roll into the required width, the film must then be perforated. Back at the start of the twentieth century, when the motion picture industry was just emerging, one of the main areas of competition between the companies seeking to dominate the market with their format was the type of perforation used. Edison used a rectangular perforation, the French a round one and most other American companies something approaching a square perforation. Around 1916, the Society of Motion Picture Engineers of America sought to standardize the perforation used throughout America: they chose to adopt the perforation that had been developed by the Bell & Howell company. This perforation had many advantages. Predominantly, it was strong and, as the dies needed to punch the perforations could easily be manufactured to a high degree of accuracy, was consistently uniform in both its positioning and size.

Howell had devised his punch by taking a piece of round drill stock 0.110 in. in diameter and grinding two parallel flats on it 0.073 in. apart, this becoming the height of the perforation. The resultant shape of Howell's perforation can be seen in Figure 6.12.

Figure 6.12 Howell's negative perforation

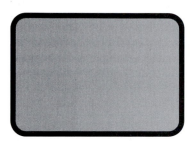

Figure 6.13 Kodak's positive perforation

One problem in the early days when nitrate base was still being used was the propensity of the base to stretch when wet in the processing chemicals and then shrink back, on drying, to a dimension smaller than it started out. This resulted in a problem when trying to contact print a shrunk negative onto an as yet unshrunk positive piece of film – they were not the same length and the perforations were now on different spacings.

The solution to this problem was to perforate the negative and positive stock with the separation of the perforations, or their pitch, initially different, so that after processing and shrinking the negative had a resultant perforation pitch the same as the unprocessed positive.

While the Bell & Howell perforation was perfect for a negative stock that requires maximum accuracy and only has to run through the camera gate once and a printing machine a few times, it was not ideal for print stock, which has to run through a projector many, many times. The problem was that, as can be seen in Figure 6.12, the join between the curved section of its shape and the straight line section results in a sharp corner, and this corner was prone to tearing after being run through a projector many times.

A different perforation was then devised, as shown in Figure 6.13, where the shape is more square and all the corners are rounded. This gives the positive perforation much more strength, though it is harder to manufacture the punches for perforating positive perforations to the same tolerances as the negative perforation. The positive perforation is known as the Kodak perforation.

Things changed with the advent of triacetate film base, as triacetate does not shrink after processing anything like as much as the old nitrate stock. The pitch of the perforations had, therefore, to be changed, so that with the new base the processed negative and the unprocessed positive had, again, the same dimensions when coming into contact in the printing machine.

You may hear reference to negatives having either long pitch, the old standard, or short pitch, the newer standard. You need not worry about this when ordering stock, as unless you make a very specific request it will always come as the modern, short pitch.

The old, long pitch is only used nowadays for very specialized applications, such as when several film strips are run through the gate of the camera at the same time – as in some forms of process photography.

For 35 mm, the consistency and accuracy of perforating is vital to the steadiness of the image. The majority of both camera and projector mechanisms in use today locate the image using only the perforations. In the camera, this is usually achieved by inserting register pins into two or four perforations after the claw has pulled down the film; they are then left in place for the duration of the exposure, being withdrawn after the shutter has closed ready for the next pull-down. In a projector mechanism, the usual arrangement is to have the film pulled through the gate by a rotating sprocket, which is locked absolutely rigid for the period the shutter is open. This is usually achieved using a device known as a Maltese cross. The benefit of using a Maltese cross mechanism in the projector is that as the film is wrapped around at least half of the sprocket, many of the perforations are used to pull the film through the gate and this mechanism is therefore very kind to the film, so that it may be shown many times without damage. The Maltese cross has not been used as a camera mechanism for perhaps 90 years, its disadvantage being that it creates quite a lot of vibration and noise. However, this is no disadvantage in a projection room isolated from the audience and where the projector is large and heavy, thus absorbing the vibration.

For 16 mm, things are a little different. While some cameras still utilize a register pin, even they usually only deploy one. Some cameras manage to give very good registration without a register pin at all. Virtually all cameras, with the exception of the Mitchell and Panaflex 16 mm cameras, use edge guides in the film gate to add accuracy to the positioning of the images on the negative. Some cameras use rigid guides both sides of the film and others use a rigid guide one side with a sprung guide the other to absorb any variation in the slit width of the film. This clearly makes the quality of the slitting process more critical in most 16 mm cameras than their 35 mm counterparts.

Edge numbers

You may have thought of the little numbers printed on the film, between the perforations, as pretty irrelevant – they are not. In fact, to certain parts of our industry, they are the very stuff of life. There are two very different functions carried out by these apparently insignificant numbers. Firstly, there is a number that doesn't change throughout the roll: this is the manufacturer's batch number, which tells you the maker, the type of film, the emulsion number, the parent roll number and the perforator number.

All this information becomes vital in the unlikely event of there being a fault in the manufacture of the stock since, by decoding the batch number, the manufacturer can not only deduce where in their factory the fault lies but, perhaps more importantly, they can immediately contact any other customer who may be about to use the same batch and replace that batch so as to prevent them shooting on possibly faulty stock.

It is vital that this batch number reaches the laboratory correctly because, until the film is developed, the batch number cannot be read as it is applied as a photographic exposure; it is therefore referred to as latent image edge signing. Years ago, some manufacturers mechanically printed the batch number on the edge of the film, but this practice is now redundant.

The second number to be printed regularly down the side of the film does not remain the same: it changes every single time it is printed. Again, it is a latent image. This number is there so that when post-production is finished, and the neg. cutters are about to cut the master negative, it is possible to match this final cut to the negative by using these numbers. Kodak, by the way, call their version of these numbers a Key Kode.

If the film has been cut in the traditional manner, by having a rush print made and physically cutting this print, then the edge numbers on the negative will be printed through onto the print stock together with the image. They can then be read off and a list of cuts made up for the neg. cutter.

By far the most common way of cutting a picture nowadays is using a non-linear computer editing machine. Here the negative will have been directly transferred to videotape and this tape will have been played into the editing computer's random access memory. At the same time, the edge numbers, or Key Kode, will have been automatically logged and their relative position will be transferred to a separate part of the computer memory.

This transfer of information is possible because every Key Kode, or its equivalent, is printed onto the negative in two forms: a string of conventional numbers (referred to as the man-readable numbers) and a bar code (just like those found in the supermarket). These bar codes can easily be read by a scanner as the negative passes through the telecine during the neg.-to-tape transfer process. These are referred to as the machine-readable numbers.

If the picture has been cut using a non-linear process such as Avid or Lightworks, then at the end of the editing, when a final cut has been agreed, the computer can be used to produce an edit decision list. The edit decision list can be transferred to a floppy disk or be printed out as hard copy. From this list it is easy to see, in one column, all the cuts as the edge sign number plus the number of frames to the actual last frame before the cut. This list is then sent to the neg. cutters to make up the final cut neg. for printing.

Care, shipping and handling

Although film stock is a fairly robust medium, certain precautions should be taken to keep it in perfect condition, especially before the image has been processed. The main threats to image quality degradation are:

1   Temperature
2   Humidity
3   Fogging from gases or radiation.

Even when kept in perfect storage conditions, it is advisable to use the film within six months of purchase. If you are travelling abroad it is worth remembering that most stock manufacturers offer a service of payment in your home country and collection from their nearest agent to your location. In this way, you are at least assured that no deterioration by any means has occurred before you start shooting.

Figure 6.14 shows the ranges of both temperature and humidity that most manufacturers recommend for storing motion picture film.

The actual speed of the film will have an effect on the rate of or susceptibility to various kinds of damage. This is particularly true of X-ray radiation, where the more sensitive the film is to visible light, the more sensitive it will be to X-rays.

When shipping undeveloped film stock, great care must be exercised to reduce the amount of X-ray radiation the stock is subjected to.

If you have to travel with your film stock always take it in hand baggage. Checked baggage that goes in the hold may receive far more radiation than hand baggage and film can be completely ruined. Take with you a changing bag and a spare, empty, film tin, together with a film bag. With luck you may be able to persuade the check-in personnel to do a hand-search of your film. This is far safer than letting it go through any X-ray machine, even if they are labelled 'Film Safe'. For our purposes it is best to assume there is no such thing as a film-safe X-ray machine.

It is often possible to ring the customs department in advance and warn them of your problem and ask for their co-operation when you get to the barrier.

	Short-term Less than 6 months		Long-term More than 6 months	
	Temperature	% Relative humidity	Temperature	% Relative humidity
Raw stock still in its original sealed cans	13°C (55°F)	Below 60%	−18 to −23°C (0–10°F)	Below 60%
Exposed but unprocessed film	−18 to −23°C (0–10°F)	Below 20%	NOT ADVISED	

Processed film:
  Black and white
  Colour
	21°C (70°F)
	21°C (70°F)
		60% or lower
		20–50%
			21°C (70°F)
			2°C (36°F)
				20–30%
				20–30%

Figure 6.14
Recommended film stock
storage conditions

The effect of X-ray radiation on your film will be cumulative. This means that the more often it is X-rayed, the more the X-ray exposure will build up until it reaches the level where it is noticeable within the image. Therefore, if you are travelling through several airports before you can have your film processed, try and get them all to hand-search your film stock. It can be very tedious, but every time you succeed you greatly reduce the chances of any noticeable X-ray fog on your negative.

An alternative is to employ a shipping agent who specializes in the film business. Because they become well known and trusted at the airport they work from, they can very often solve your problems very easily. The manufacturer of the particular stock you are using will most likely be able to advise you as to reliable shipping agents in the areas through which you are planning to travel.

As to deterioration through excessive temperature and humidity, common sense is all that is needed to avoid any problems. By looking at Figure 6.14 you can check the parameters that are acceptable. If you are likely to be going to parts of the world where you may encounter a problem, then any photographic shop specializing in darkroom equipment will sell you a robust thermometer and hygrometer at very little cost; you can then use these to keep a check on matters. In extremely hot conditions, you may be able to negotiate with the hotel chef to put the majority of your stock in a fridge. A good quality cool bag (the Australians call it an 'Esky') should be used for the stock you need that day only. It is most important that you let any film that has been in a fridge come up to temperature before you load it into a magazine – if you don't, condensation will form. If the nights are reasonably cool, then take the film from the fridge late in the evening and put it into your cool bag first thing in the morning.

However careful you have been while travelling, always have the film processed as soon as possible after exposure. If you are really worried about any adverse effects, you might consider having the film processed in the country you are working in. If the laboratory seems reasonably good, you can always send a test roll in before committing the majority of your rushes to them. Again, asking your stock supplier will usually elicit an opinion, albeit a guarded one, as to the reliability of any laboratory.

7
Basic sensitometry

For some reason, most film technicians find sensitometry either boring or frightening. This is unfortunate, since with only a basic knowledge of the photographic process and the ability to do your two times table, you can master all you need to know to gain considerably more control over your picture making.

Sensitometry, as the word would suggest, is the technique we use for measuring and evaluating the sensitivity of a film emulsion to light. The important part of the evaluation, to cinematographers, is to know how much light arriving at the emulsion is needed to produce the required density of image on the film after development. The relationship between the amount of light, the exposure and the darkening, the density, will not be in the same ratio over the entire range of brightness recorded on the film. This is important, since in creating the mood of the final picture the cinematographer will be very concerned to know how much detail will be seen in the shadowed part of the image and, particularly if outdoors, will wish to know the details that can be recorded in the highlights of the scene so as to know if sky, sand, snow, etc. will be represented faithfully in the picture. It is in the shadows and the highlights that the response becomes non-linear.

In order to understand the relationship between exposure and density, we commonly plot a graph of the relationship between the two. Figure 7.1 shows a graph of exposure plotted against density. Unfortunately, the sections of the graph crucial to the cinematographer, the beginning and end of the curve, which represent the shadows and the highlights, are nearly vertical and horizontal respectively and are therefore virtually meaningless.

In 1890, two researchers, Hurter and Driffield, carried out detailed experiments into the various characteristics of film emulsions. An important outcome of these investigations was the realization that a curve relating resultant image density to exposure could be redrawn with the horizontal axis representing not exposure but, quite simply, the logarithm of exposure. This produced a much more useful curve, as shown in Figure 7.2. This curve, which is now universally used, is more practical for camera exposure as it now alters by a factor that is geometric not arithmetic. For instance, when we increase the exposure time from one-hundredth of a second to one-fiftieth of a second, we speak

Figure 7.1 Density plotted against exposure measured in metre-candle-seconds

Figure 7.2 Density plotted against the logarithm of exposure

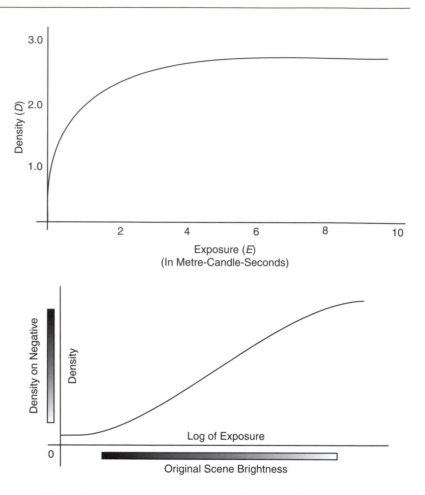

of doubling the exposure, not increasing it by another one-hundredth of a second. Hurter and Driffield's logarithmic curve therefore gives a very reasonable representation of the way in which density increases when the exposure is increased.

For many years the type of curve shown in Figure 7.2 was referred to as the H and D curve in recognition of Hurter and Driffield, who devised it. Nowadays, it is almost always referred to as a sensitometric curve or as a film's characteristic curve – because that is what it describes, the characteristics of the emulsion.

There are several useful pieces of information that can be derived from a characteristic curve. Firstly, and most importantly for 80 per cent of our image is the middle section of the curve that, somewhat contrary to its name, should be almost straight. Any scene brightnesses that fall on this section of the curve will produce densities that have a straightforward relationship to any other brightnesses falling on this straight-line section. It is therefore very easy to know, over this section of the curve, which scene brightnesses produce what densities.

The ends of the curve in Figure 7.3 are clearly curved. At the lower curved section, which we refer to as the toe of the curve, the straight-line section progressively flattens out until it becomes horizontal. As you can see from the brightness wedge below the graph, this is where we will be recording the shadow detail. As, emotionally, the audience

Figure 7.3 Densities produced
on the negative as they relate
to original scene brightness

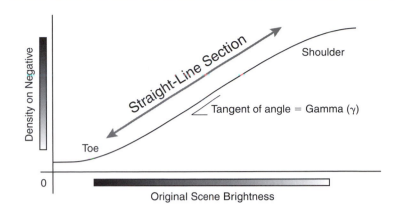

will have a greater interest in what is going on in the shadows, a knowledge of the type and shape of this toe of the curve for the film we are using can give the cinematographer a greater command of their storytelling powers. At the other, higher, end of the curve, where the highlights are going to be recorded, again the straight line rounds off to the horizontal; this section of the characteristic curve we call the shoulder.

There is another important aspect of the characteristic curve in which we, as cinematographers, need to take an interest. It is commonly referred to as the gamma of the emulsion and is represented by the Greek letter of that name – γ. The gamma is the measurement of the rate of change of the densities created as the exposure changes. It is, in fact, a very simple measurement. One simply measures the angle of the straight-line section of the characteristic curve to the horizontal and takes the tangent of this angle from a scientific calculator or a set of logarithmic tables – the resultant figure is the gamma.

The tangent of 45° is 1; therefore, a characteristic curve with a straight-line section of 45° will have a γ of 1. In this case, there will be a straight 1:1 relationship between exposure and resultant density.

The speed of the film, or how sensitive to light it is, is often referred to as its ASA speed. This speed rating comes from a formula devised by the American Standards Association, hence ASA speed, but is now more commonly referred to as a film's ISO (International Standards Organization). The number usually remains the same. In sensitometric terms, films of differing sensitivity, or speed, can be expected to have their characteristic curve in a different position on the graph paper. Figure 7.4 shows three films that only have one differing characteristic – their speed or sensitivity.

In Figure 7.4, the dotted lines show the different exposures required to produce the same density on different negatives. The pale line represents a slow film having a low ASA speed. To produce the required density, this film needs a lot of light or a bright part of the scene. The medium-speed film, shown as the middle of the three curves, requires less exposure to produce the required density and the high-speed film on the left of the three requires very little. The high-speed film therefore will produce a medium density from a reasonably dark object, whereas the slow film would need to be looking at a much brighter object to produce the same resultant density.

Another characteristic the cinematographer needs to be aware of is the relative contrast of the film in use. Contrast and gamma are often

Figure 7.4 D–log E curve
showing the effect of changing
the speed of the emulsion

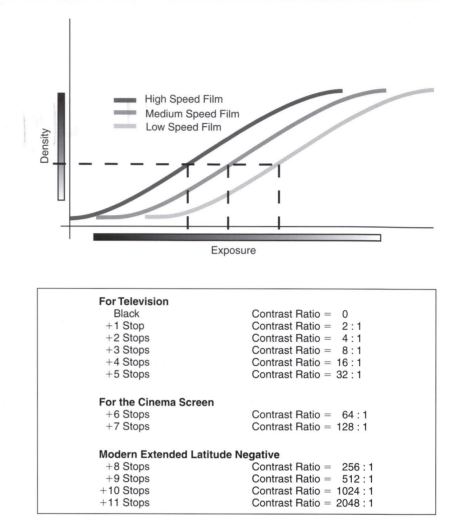

Figure 7.5 Contrast ratios
for various delivery systems

For Television

Black	Contrast Ratio = 0
+1 Stop	Contrast Ratio = 2 : 1
+2 Stops	Contrast Ratio = 4 : 1
+3 Stops	Contrast Ratio = 8 : 1
+4 Stops	Contrast Ratio = 16 : 1
+5 Stops	Contrast Ratio = 32 : 1

For the Cinema Screen

+6 Stops	Contrast Ratio = 64 : 1
+7 Stops	Contrast Ratio = 128 : 1

Modern Extended Latitude Negative

+8 Stops	Contrast Ratio = 256 : 1
+9 Stops	Contrast Ratio = 512 : 1
+10 Stops	Contrast Ratio = 1024 : 1
+11 Stops	Contrast Ratio = 2048 : 1

confused. As we have seen, gamma is a measurement of the rate of change of the exposure–density relationship. Contrast refers to the brightness range and the gradation between the highlights and the shadows; it is therefore expressed as a ratio. For instance, a television picture, even on a perfectly set-up screen, will only be able to show a brightness range equivalent to five stops of exposure; it will therefore have a contrast range of 32:1, as shown in Figure 7.5. The contrast range that can be shown on a first-class cinema screen is the equivalent of seven stops of exposure. Recently, developments in the construction of camera negative emulsions have made it possible to manufacture a negative able to record the equivalent of 10 stops of brightness; this gives the film a contrast ratio of an incredible 1024:1. The value of this range to the working cinematographer is discussed in Chapter 11.

Despite the definitions above, we still think of a 'contrasty' film as one having severe blacks and whites with little information in the mid-tones. This kind of image would probably be described in sensitometric terms as having a high gamma, i.e. one having a steep straight-line section, as shown in Figure 7.6. It would, in all probability, have a low

Figure 7.6 The effect of changing the gamma of an emulsion

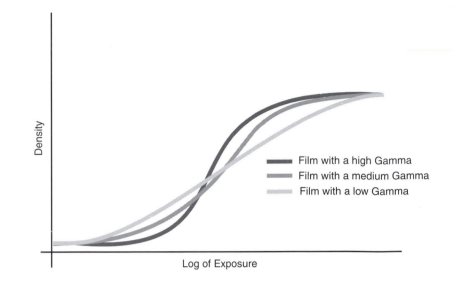

contrast ratio. As can be seen by comparing the curves in Figure 7.6, by increasing the gamma and steepening the curve the usable straight-line section relates to a shorter distance along the exposure axis, thus the contrast ratio will be lower. We must learn to recognize the difference between contrast expressed as a ratio and apparent contrast as a 'soot and whitewash' image.

In all the graphs shown in this chapter you will see that the curve never reaches zero on the vertical density line. This is because the film can never be made absolutely clear, i.e. having a density of zero. This is mainly the result of two things:

1   The base material it is coated on is not completely clear.
2   When film is manufactured it receives an almost imperceptible exposure from things other than light. The film emulsion is very slightly sensitive to pressure, heat, etc. and therefore the actual process of manufacture causes a very slight darkening.

The resultant small density at the very bottom of the curve we therefore call the base level fog.

8
The laboratory

The laboratory contact

The laboratory contact person (always referred to as the 'lab contact') is one of the more important people in a DP's life. Every morning, usually somewhere between 7.30 and 8.00, a member of the camera crew will be detailed to phone the lab. This is to obtain the report on yesterday's rushes, or dailies as they are known in the USA. The report will contain information as to how well the contact thought the overall look of the rushes had been achieved, an accurate list of any hairs or scratches with precise slate numbers and the all-important printer lights. The printer lights are usually given in the order of red, green and blue with, often, an average of all three colours for each scene or roll. This is known as an overall light and is an expression of the overall exposure.

The overall exposure figure will only be of use if you have been working under normal lighting conditions. If you have been shifting your colours using the grey scale or, for instance, shooting under fluorescent lighting, you will need to interpret the RGB (Red, Green, Blue) numbers.

Your laboratory contact will have been responsible for setting the grading lights the night before and can therefore have a huge effect on the look of the DP's work. For this reason, it is always wise to talk to the lab contact before starting a picture; this way they know what you are trying to achieve. For the same reason, I always try and make that early morning call myself, not just to get a feel for yesterday's work but to discuss what we are going to be shooting today, so the contact has some idea of what I had in mind when they come to grade the negative in the small hours of the morning.

If you are working on one set for several days, it is a good idea to invite the lab contact on to the set. They spend so much of their life in the dark they are usually only too grateful for the chance of a visit. More importantly, it lets them see the real thing and this makes their involvement in the production all the more real.

Figure 8.1 Schematic diagram
of the Bell & Howell Model C
printer light source

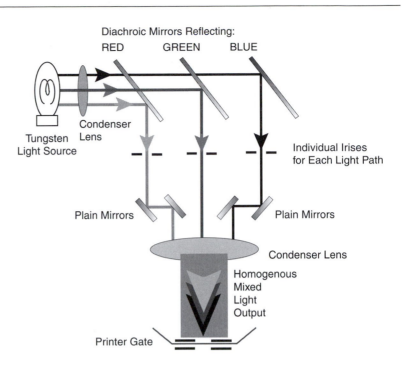

Printer lights

The printer lights quoted by the lab are derived from the first printing machine that had a truly successful light source with which to control a mixture of red, green and blue lights within very fine degrees. This was, and is, the Bell & Howell Model C printer.

Figure 8.1 shows a schematic diagram of the Model C's light source. White light from a simple tungsten source is first put through a condenser lens so as to form an organized beam. The beam of light then arrives at a diachroic mirror, which will reflect red light but is transparent to green and blue light. The beam continues until it reaches the second mirror, which will only reflect green light and is transparent to blue light. The beam continues further to the last mirror, which will only reflect blue light.

All of the individual beams, one each for these three colours, now pass through their own, separate iris. Each iris is identical and has 50 carefully graduated settings, where the difference between all the settings is usually equivalent to one-sixth of a stop on a camera lens.

Using simple mirrors, and a second condenser lens, all the three colours are then recombined into a homogeneous light source. This light source then delivers its beam to the printer gate.

If all three irises controlling the individual primary colours were set to their middle position, light 25 on the scale, then pure white light would be delivered to the printer's gate. Things are so arranged that this would also, normally, be the perfect exposure for a perfectly exposed negative being printed onto a standard print stock. We would then know that if the laboratory reported RGB printer lights of 25,25,25, our negative was perfectly exposed and had printed most satisfactorily.

Figure 8.2 The contact printer

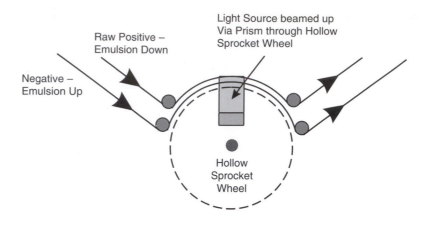

Not all negatives have exactly the same colour balance, and neither do all print stocks. It is therefore important, before you start a picture, to ask the contact person what they would consider to be the perfect printer lights for the combination of negative and positive film stocks you are going to be using. If you are shooting for television only, and producing your final transmission tape directly from the negative, they may suggest slightly higher printer lights – that is, the negative should be given a little more exposure, as this usually suits the telecine machines and delivers a better overall feel to the television picture.

It is important to remember that a variation of six printer lights more or less relates to one stop of exposure on the camera. Do check with the actual laboratory you are going to use, as some will use six lights to a stop and some use eight.

Contact printing

Nearly all rushes prints are made on high-speed contact printing machines. These are very much like the schematic diagram (Figure 8.2), where a light source similar to the Bell & Howell Model C described above delivers its output via a prism to the centre of a hollow sprocket wheel. Wrapped around that sprocket is, on the inside, the processed negative with its emulsion facing upwards. Wrapped on the outside of that is the raw positive stock with its emulsion facing inwards. The emulsions of the two films are therefore in direct contact.

This simple and very effective arrangement enables the laboratory to print the rushes overnight at very high speed. This is essential since all the productions they are handling every night will expect their reports first thing in the morning.

Because the image on the negative emulsion is in direct contact with the emulsion on the positive, a contact print will be of very high optical quality.

Optical printers

Figure 8.3 shows the layout of an optical printer. Optical printers are very different from contact printers. Both the negative and the positive are held in independent gates and are simultaneously moved

Figure 8.3 The optical printer

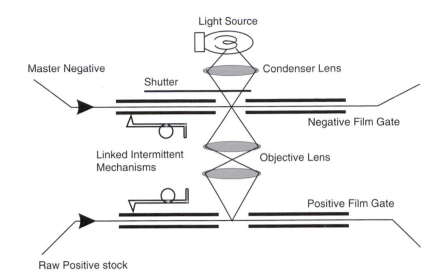

through these gates one frame at a time by linked intermittent mechanisms. In order to transfer the image from the negative to the positive film, an objective lens is positioned between the two gates.

The purpose of this layout is to enable optical effects, such as fades and dissolves, to be achieved. A dissolve is made by first printing the outgoing shot and fading out the printer light. The positive film is then rewound and the incoming shot replaces the outgoing shot. The printer is then restarted and the light source faded in over the same section of print stock. This produces a situation where the outgoing image is reduced in exposure at exactly the place on the positive where the incoming exposure is increasing. Therefore, the overall exposure from the two negatives always adds up to the full, correct, exposure.

Although an optical printer can achieve many elegant effects, it does have two distinct disadvantages. Firstly, because it has, by its very needs and design, an intermittent mechanism, it cannot be run at anything like the speed of the contact printer. Therefore, optical prints will always cost considerably more than contact prints because of the extra machine time. Secondly, although the objective lenses used in optical printers are always of the very highest quality, often being specially computed for the task, nevertheless no optical path, even if it only contained air, will ever produce a print as perfect as one made with the two emulsions in absolute contact.

The cinematographer must be aware that there will be two slight differences in the appearance of a contact print and an optical print. Due to the optical path travelled by the image between the two emulsions in an optical printer, there must be a slight loss of definition compared with a contact print. This is hardly worth worrying about, as the loss is very, very slight. The second important effect of the optical printer is to introduce a little flare, again as a result of there being an objective lens between the two emulsions. Flare is simply a very small amount of the total amount of light forming the image being lost to the image and redistributed, evenly, over the whole of the image. The effect of this is to add a small percentage of the overall image to all the tones in the image. In Figure 8.4, the effect of flare has been greatly exaggerated in order to

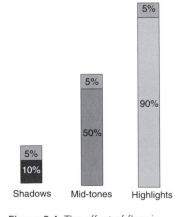

Figure 8.4 The effect of flare in an optical printer

make a graphic representation and the matter more understandable. If we look at the three sections of the tonal range shown, a shadow representing 10 per cent of the total exposure, a mid-tone representing 50 per cent of the exposure and a highlight representing 90 per cent of the overall exposure, then how will each be affected by flare?

To make this example clear, let us assume that the overall flare is 5 per cent of the total exposure and add this to each of the tones. The highlight will increase in brightness to 95 per cent of the maximum brightness, not a huge, relative, change. If we add 5 per cent of overall brightness to the mid-tone of 50 per cent, we will arrive at a total brightness of 55 per cent, a reasonable but bearable change. If we now add 5 per cent of total brightness to the shadow, which only starts with a 10 per cent brightness, then we find a new total brightness of 15 per cent. As this is half as much again as the original shadow brightness, it will be very noticeable indeed and will show in two ways. The density of the shadows will now appear higher and less menacing. The information in the shadows will appear to be reduced, as only two-thirds of the shadow exposure is now original scene. One-third is just a flat, even, background exposure. This often produces the unattractive shadows we hear described as having 'milky blacks'.

The example of 5 per cent of total brightness becoming flare in an optical printer has been used to make the point clearer. In a worst case scenario, it is unlikely that printer flare will ever amount to 1 per cent of maximum scene brightness, but even so that can be a relatively important factor, particularly in a low-key scene where most of the important parts of the image will be at brightness of less than 20 per cent of the total available.

If you are making a feature film where the image may well be printed through an optical printer several times (see the section 'Cinema release prints' later in this chapter), and you intend to use a reasonable amount of diffusion in front of the camera, then you may wish to have just one roll of tests printed up right through the internegative/interpositive process in order to satisfy yourself that the amount of diffusion you are using is correct for the release print, not the contact printed rushes. This, as we have seen, is particularly important on low-key scenes, where printer flare becomes a noticeable factor.

When a cinematographer complains that they never got a release print as good as the rushes, it is most likely that they were shooting a low-key picture, with very thin, underexposed negatives. These thin negatives will have allowed a lot of flare to build up in the optical printing of the release prints and this will not have shown in the contact prints. This is the strongest argument I know for always making a fully exposed negative, even on a low-key scene.

Negative cutting

Some laboratories will take on the task of cutting the original negative and others prefer the work to go out to a specialist company. It is a very skilled task and should never be undertaken until the final cut of the film has been approved by the producers and has been 'locked off'.

The negative is either cut to match the edge numbers of the cut rushes or, almost universally now, cut to match the edit decision list (EDL) generated by a non-linear computer editing process such as Avid or Lightworks. The EDL may be delivered to the neg. cutters

Figure 8.5 A and B roll negative cutting

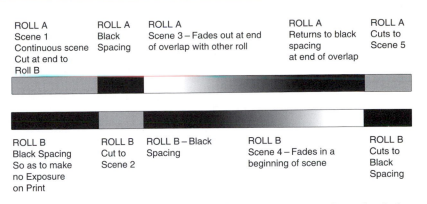

ROLL A
Scene 1
Continuous scene
Cut at end to
Roll B

ROLL A
Black
Spacing

ROLL A
Scene 3 – Fades out at end
of overlap with other roll

ROLL A
Returns to black
spacing
at end of overlap

ROLL A
Cuts to
Scene 5

ROLL B
Black Spacing
So as to make
no Exposure
on Print

ROLL B
Cut to
Scene 2

ROLL B – Black
Spacing

ROLL B
Scene 4 – Fades in a
beginning of scene

ROLL B
Cuts to
Black
Spacing

on a paper printout or a computer floppy disk, or perhaps both for safety.

If a print is required then the negative will be cut in the format known as an A and B roll. The principal of A and B roll neg. cutting is that you put all the odd shot numbers on one roll of film with black spacing between each shot. You then make up another roll of film with all the even numbered shots on it, again with black spacing in between. On both rolls you make the spacing the same length as the missing shot, which is on the other roll.

You can vary this technique to let two shots overlap, so that a dissolve can be created when the two rolls are printed one after the other.

Figure 8.5 shows how the A and B rolls might be laid out. The first shot of the film is on the top roll, roll A. This roll is printed to the positive first. When the shot comes to an end, black spacing is cut on and thus there will be no exposure on the positive.

When the second roll is printed to the positive there will be no exposure from it during shot 1, as it only consists of black spacing. At exactly the frame where the exposure from roll A ends, the exposure from roll B will start. In this way, one gets a continuous, single length of film with all the cuts printed onto it.

The sequence continues as scene 3, being an odd-numbered scene, gets printed at exactly the point where scene 2 on roll B ends. At the end of scene 3, the editor has decided to have a dissolve to scene 4. The scenes have therefore to overlap; scene 3 continues longer on roll A before being cut to black. The incoming scene, scene 4, must start exactly the same amount earlier. When printing scene 3 from roll A the printer will fade to black for, say, 20 frames. If a 20-frame dissolve has been decided upon, then scene 4 on roll B will start 20 frames early and, when printed, will fade in to full exposure for those 20 frames and remain at full exposure until the end of that shot.

The cut negative will therefore consist of two rolls of identical length. Roll A will contain all the odd-numbered shots and roll B all the even-numbered shots. Where no exposure is required from one of the rolls there will be black spacing. When both rolls have been printed, one after the other, the result will be the whole film on a single roll with no physical joins.

Cinema release prints

Making cinema release prints is a somewhat protracted business, made so by the need for many release prints, possibly in the hundreds for worldwide distribution, all of which must originate from the single camera negative. Even if one were prepared to try and print all the release prints from the camera negative, it would simply not be mechanically strong enough to make that many prints.

What is needed therefore are a number of duplicate negatives, of very high quality, from each of which a sensible number of prints can be made, or 'struck' as the process is often referred to.

The process starts with the A and B roll cut negative. This will be graded and a trial print will be struck; this is known as the first answer print. It may take several answer prints before the director, the DP, the producer and the laboratory are all happy with the finished result. When they are happy a fine grain, graded, interpositive will be struck. From the interpositive, an internegative will be struck and a print made from this and checked by all concerned. This process is shown in Figure 8.6.

If the test print from the first internegative is considered to be all that is expected, then further internegatives will be made. From each of these internegatives many release prints can be struck.

It is in everyone's interest that the camera negative, now cut as A and B rolls, must be run through a printer as rarely as possible, for it now represents the whole of the producer's investment. There is much relief when a successful internegative has been struck, since only then, for the first time, is there an alternative to the master camera negative should something unfortunate happen to that master.

On very big budget pictures, when all the required internegatives have been approved and, perhaps, a safety copy of the original inter-positive has been made, a single print may be struck from the camera original A and B roll cut negatives. This is known as the premier copy and will be used for the one-off showings at international premieres. As we have seen in the earlier part of this chapter, there is a slight loss of quality as the image goes through the various prints and negatives that come between the camera negative and a normal release print. In order to make the premiere showing as special as possible, these pre-miere prints will occasionally be struck.

The 'long-handled' negative cut

When shooting film destined only for television transmission, many people believe the finest quality is achieved by directly transferring the camera negative to a digital master tape. If the negative has been exposed with this in mind, I am a great advocate of this process.

Providing a print is never going to be required, then the A and B roll neg. cut can be a hindrance rather than an asset. In order to transfer an A and B roll cut, each roll must go through a telecine machine on its own, which produces two master tapes that are automatically, using the EDL, conformed into a single master tape. The disadvantage is that it is very difficult to grade the film when you cannot see the shots one after another.

If both a print and a neg. transfer are required, a compromise is usually to grade the A and B rolls as best you can, conform the tape and have a final grading session from tape to tape. This has a huge disadvantage for the cinematographer. Once the image is transferred to tape there are only the five stops of the tonal range of television to work with. Tape-to-tape

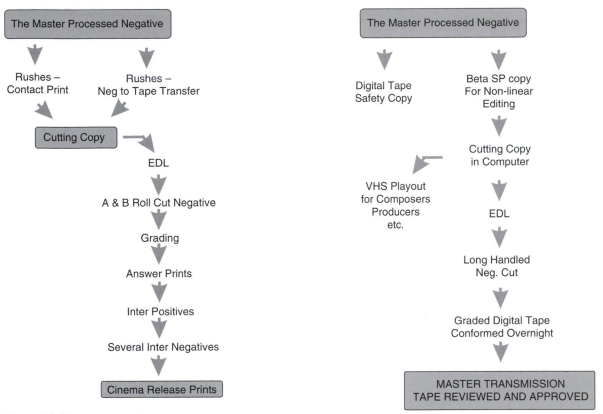

Figure 8.6 The route to a cinema release print

Figure 8.7 The route to a graded master transmission tape

grading, in my opinion, makes the final image look more and more like a video original – if this happens, why did you go to all the trouble and expense of producing a high-quality film master?

To overcome this, a different way of neg. cutting has been devised. The flow chart (Figure 8.7) shows the process used. The negative is assembled as a single roll. At each join, a few extra frames are left attached to the shots so that any damage that might occur during the physical cutting of the negative is nowhere near the frames to be printed. The film is graded at a single pass; admittedly, the cuts are a little strange, but this does not seem to be a great problem.

The digital tape resulting from a single roll grading is, again, conformed to the correct cuts using the EDL, as before. This usually happens overnight. The following day you check the result, which is usually perfect. If further adjustments are deemed necessary they are usually so slight that a tape-to-tape regrade will not, in these circumstances, be noticeable. If major changes are required it is very easy to spin the single roll negative down to the appropriate scene and make a completely new grade. This is then conformed and cut in to the original tape master in an on-line editing suite.

Because of the extra bits of scene that must be left on the shots as the single roll negative is made up, this has become known as a long-handled neg. cut – the handles being the extra bits top and tail of each shot.

Film grading

It is quite common to find in a DP's contract either for a cinema film or a major television drama a clause stating that, subject to their availability, they will be asked to attend, indeed usually supervise, the grading at the laboratory. This is the moment for the cinematographer to add the final polish to the film.

The process usually takes the form of the DP and the grader from the laboratory sitting in a viewing theatre and looking at the cut rush print, and from this deciding what changes they wish to make in order to strike the first answer print overnight from an A and B roll cut negative. This answer print will be viewed the following morning and may, with luck, be perfectly acceptable. More likely, at least a second answer print is needed. If too many answer prints are ordered, then beware, the producer may start to question the quality of your master negative or whether you are being just a little too fussy and consequently spending too much of their post-production budget.

The film grader will be taking notes during the viewing in order to be sure of the changes the DP wants. These notes are most often a plus or minus sign in front of a printer point change number with the colour shown. A very experienced DP may be able to communicate with the grader directly in printer points, but this is not essential nor always preferable. It is quite acceptable to ask for a picture to be a little more green, say, or less magenta – which, though technically being similar, sound different and might communicate better your impression of what is needed. Asking for a little more warmth is also perfectly acceptable. Remember, graders are very experienced and very much on your side, so just about any means of communicating your feelings of how you wish your pictures to look is fine. It can be hard to communicate feelings with printer light numbers.

Unfortunately, there is one absolute fact attached to film grading – if it's not on the negative there is nothing you can do to get it onto the print. You can only change the brightness of three colours as they pass through the negative on their way to the print stock. You cannot, as in still photography, modify in any way the contrast of the print stock or, other than in exceptional and expensive circumstances, change the way the print will be developed.

Telecine grading

All film, from whatever source, that is to be shown on television must be converted from a real image on celluloid to an electronic image stored on videotape. This is achieved by passing the film through a device called a telecine machine. Simply, this scans the real film image in the format to be transmitted, say 625 lines in the UK and 525 lines in the USA, and then this signal is recorded onto a conventional videotape machine.

Between the telecine machine and the videotape machine is a control desk, with which many adjustments to the image may be performed. The telecine can, by the flick of a switch, be converted from transferring a positive image from a photographic print to transferring from the master negative, inverting the image to a positive electronically so that the grading and recording are both a positive image.

Telecine grading is, for me at least, one of the more enjoyable parts of the film-making process. It is akin to being a cabinet maker who, having spent weeks or months making a beautiful piece of furniture, in one day puts the final polish on their work and all is finished.

More often than not, you sit in a room with subdued lighting, all is clean and comfortable and usually a telecine machine sits quietly behind a glass door in an air-conditioned environment. Before you is a large desk, above which are some high-grade television monitors. On the desk are the controls, which will modify your picture in almost any way you wish.

While the rule, if it's not on the negative there is nothing you can do to get it on to the print, still applies in all other respects, you can do just as much to the image as you could in a still photography dark-room, if not more, and you can do it instantly!

A first-class modern telecine grading suite can not only change the colours, as at the chemical laboratory, but can modify the gamma of the overall image or just modify the gamma of one colour. It might be possible to select one area of colour, a pure blue sky say, and work on the density, colour and gamma of that area alone. This gives the DP many more tools if you know that the finished picture will be delivered only on tape. For instance, day-for-night, always a daunting prospect, becomes much more achievable via a good telecine suite than when you only have a pure photographic process at your disposal.

Do heed the warning, though: it is only wise to use all these tricks if you are never going to produce a print as well. If you are, and you go to telecine first, many important people might be very disappointed with the print if they have already seen your highly modified telecine transfer.

The telecine process has come a long way. When I first became a DP at the BBC, film was transmitted live as it went through the telecine machine and only for a major drama production would the DP be allowed to attend a telecine rehearsal. Now it is often in our contract to telecine grade our work if that is what is required. For some years now, it has been popular to transfer the master negative directly to tape. Early telecine machines were really lined up for the response of positive film and, although the image could be inverted from a negative to a positive, many DPs and producers thought the image more filmic if the transfer was made from a print, and in those days they were probably right.

Things have come a long way. A recent film I transferred was from the negative via a C-Reality telecine scanning at 2000 lines working in a digital domain. This resolution was maintained right through the transfer desk, the latest Da Vinci, and only down-converted to 625 lines just before display on the monitor and recording on a digital tape machine. The quality was stunning. It would be a huge achievement if it were possible, at an economical price, to grade a film for theatrical release this way and make a print from that grade. This can now be achieved via digital intermediates, often referred to as DI.

9
Digital intermediates

Why turn a photographic image into digits?

Working through the photographic process from an exposed camera negative to a cinema release print is a well-known process, discussed in the previous chapter, and works exceptionally well. Likewise, the scanning of a film negative, or print, so that it may be shown on television is a well-established procedure and has become very reliable.

Scanning and grading a photographic image for television transmission has some advantages over simply making a photographic print since, in addition to the ability to alter the red, green and blue components of the picture, together with overall density, it is easy, electronically, to alter the yellow, cyan and magenta components, as well as make considerable changes to the overall contrast. Up until recently, it was impossible to take the electronically scanned image, together with any changes made, and return these changes to a photographic cinema print without a serious loss in quality. This has now changed.

The first step needed was to have a way of writing an electronic image back to film with sufficient quality for it to be indistinguishable from a conventional cinema print – the Arri Laser Printer, and some others, now offer this capability.

The second step was the introduction of devices that can scan a master camera negative with such subtlety that there was no loss in picture quality between the photographic original and the resultant electronic image.

Thirdly, the post-production suites, that had for some time been used to grade photographic images intended for transmission on television, have had their resolution and colour depth improved to such an extent that they are able to process images well up to full 35 mm film quality.

So, with these three advances it is now possible to scan a camera negative, make it into an electronic image, manipulate that image and write it back to a piece of film with such finesse that the audience will not be able to tell the difference between a print made by the traditional photo mechanical process and one that has been worked on by an electronic process.

But entering the electronic world and returning from it is an expensive process, so why would we bother? Because, in addition to greater fineness in the grading process, we can manipulate the image in other ways that can improve our storytelling abilities.

The next trick was to find electronic processes that do not degrade the image quality in any way, no matter how many times you re-record them, and this is where digital encoding comes in.

The copies of a camera master negative, in the traditional photo-chemical process, are called intermediates. As in the previous chapter, we have seen how intermediate positives and intermediate negatives are used to allow several generations of copies to be made so that a cinema release print can be produced. If these intermediates are now to be replaced by digitally encoded images, it comes as no surprise that this process has become known as a digital intermediate, or DI as it is most often referred to.

What do we mean by 'digital'?

In order to create a digital image we break up the picture into very small elements or pixels. The output from each pixel, depending on its brightness, is given a number and this number is then recorded as a code. In order to make up a full colour image, just as in the photo-graphic process, there are three separate sections of these codes, one relating to the red part of the image, one to the green and one to the blue. The number of options available for different brightnesses recorded by each pixel will significantly affect the quantity of the resultant picture. More options will give a finer picture with a smoother tone range, very like using a finer grain film.

If you give each small element of the picture, the pixel, the option to have 1000 differences between recording a black part of an image and a white part, you will get a reasonably fine picture, but if it were pos-sible to break up the tonal range from each pixel into, say, 4000 options, then the result would give a much smoother transition between the various tones in the resulting image.

Even to record a decent image comparable with 35 mm film, we are going to need something like 2000 pixels across the width of the pic-ture and around 1000 pixels vertically. That's 2 000 000 pixels per frame and, as we want to give each pixel at least 1000 options of brightness, the total number of options we will need to record will be 2 000 000 000. So far, we have only recorded one of the three necessary colours, so for a full colour single frame we need 6 000 000 000 options. At 24 frames per second, we are going to need to have a huge record-ing ability unless we can find a way to simplify matters.

The binary code

A binary code employs a combination of zeros and ones in an organ-ized way to write any value. The numbers of zeros and ones used determines how many options you will have available.

Just one option allows you to write two numbers, as zero will repre-sent a number and one will represent another. Yet if we go up just one step further and allow two options of zeros and ones we can now record four different numbers, for we have the options of 00, 01, 10 and 11. This we call a two-bit code, where two bits of information are

1-bit	0 (or 1) 2 = 2 values
2-bit	0 1 2 × 2 = 4 values
4-bit	0 1 0 1 2 × 2 × 2 × 2 = 16 values
6-bit	0 1 0 1 0 1 2 × 2 × 2 × 2 × 2 × 2 = 64 values
8-bit	0 1 0 1 0 1 0 1 2 × 2 × 2 × 2 × 2 × 2 × 2 × 2 = 256 values
10-bit	0 1 0 1 0 1 0 1 0 1 2 × 2 × 2 × 2 × 2 × 2 × 2 × 2 × 2 × 2 = 1024 values
12-bit	0 1 0 1 0 1 0 1 0 1 0 1 2 × 2 × 2 × 2 × 2 × 2 × 2 × 2 × 2 × 2 × 2 × 2 = 4096 values

Figure 9.1 The effect of adding more bits to the binary code

used to write four combinations, with each combination representing one value.

The great advantage of this system is that one can easily design a machine, or electronic circuit, to recognize this code, as we can tell it one is represented by 'On' and zero is represented by 'Off'. So, as we are only asking our machine to tell if it is on or off to understand all the numbers we require, we have gained a huge advantage – we can copy our string of codes as many times as we like, with absolute accuracy, and even the most stupid of machines can tell if it is on or off.

Here lies the advantage of digital copying over photographic copying; every time you make a photographic copy there will be some loss in quality, no matter how small, but every digital copy should be an exact replica of the original. We can now, therefore, make as many copies, or intermediates, as we wish.

But how many combinations of zeros and ones should we assign to each pixel to get an exact representation of our photographic original? Well, perceived wisdom tells us we need 10 or 12 combinations of zeros and ones in order that the digital intermediate process remains seamless. Figure 9.1 shows how the number of combinations available with different numbers of zeros and ones moves up to an astounding 4096 for 12-bit encoding.

Linear and logarithmic sampling

There is a way of encoding the original scanning of the camera negative that can both make the picture more appealing to the eye and, at the same time, reduce the size of the digital files used to store the images. It involves the use of logarithmic sampling rather than the traditional linear sampling.

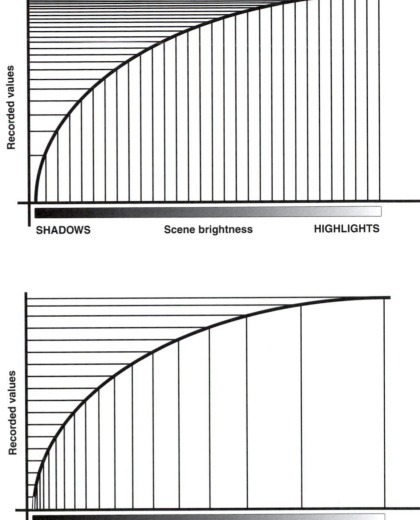

Figure 9.2 Screen brightness using linear sampling

Figure 9.3 Screen brightness using logarithmic sampling

With linear sampling, the steps between each brightness sampled are exactly the same throughout the tonal range of the master image, as in Figure 9.2. Because of the shape of the brightness response curve, a finer gradation between recorded values will occur in the highlights than in the shadows. With logarithmic sampling, as shown in Figure 9.3, there are more steps in the area of the shadowed part of the scene than in the highlights, and this results in the recorded values being evenly spaced across the tonal range.

There is another advantage to logarithmic sampling. Original camera negative will usually have an overall density range of 2.0D from the clearest part of the film to the darkest. The industry standard Kodak specified Cineon (.CIN) film file format for digital recording, the most widely used in the DI world, works on the basis that between each digital sample there will be a density change of 0.002D on the camera negative. If we sample in a linear pattern, the 11-stop dynamic range of a modern camera negative will need a 13-bit file to hold all that data using 0.002 intervals of density between samples. This means that, in order to get sufficient data for the shadows to look real, there must be 8192 options of recordable brightness for each pixel.

However, if a tonal range of 11 stops on the camera negative is sampled in a logarithmic way, the same amount of necessary information can be recorded on a 10-bit file, which has only 1024 options. This means much smaller files are needed but the audience will still see an image of equivalent quality.

Image acquisition

At the start of the DI process it is necessary to scan the photographic image so that we can write it in the binary code. The most important decision is what digital resolution we use and this is described by referring to the number of pixels the horizontal width of the picture is broken up into. There is much discussion in the post-production world as to how many horizontal pixels are needed, with almost as many opinions as there are post-production houses, so I am going to give my opinion, and I have taken very good advice on this.

A 35 mm master camera negative is almost universally agreed to have the equivalent of a digital image of 4000 pixels horizontally. Therefore, if you wish to take a shot, manipulate it digitally and return it to the cut camera master negative, you must scan at 4000 pixel resolution in order that no discernible degradation in picture quality occurs when you make the photographic intermediates.

If you are going to scan your camera master and do all your intermediates digitally, only returning to film for the release print, or at the worst the intermediate photographic negative, then scanning your original at 2000 pixels horizontally will be enough and can produce an image on the cinema screen every bit as good as the purely photographic method described above.

Incidentally, we refer to a picture with 4000 horizontal pixels as having a 4k resolution and one with 2000 pixels as 2k.

Why the difference? The traditional route from camera master negative to the cinema release print usually looks like this:

1   Camera negative – printed to intermediate positives.
2   Intermediate positive – printed to intermediate negatives.
3   Intermediate negatives – printed to cinema release prints.
4   Cinema release print – to cinema screen.

It is an inescapable fact that every time you make a photographic copy you must lose some picture quality; therefore, if you go through this process starting with 4k camera negative you will end up on the screen with something having a poorer resolution.

To satisfy the resolution of an audience sitting in the optimum viewing position in a cinema, the screen picture quality must have a horizontal resolution equivalent to 1000 pixels or better. Only then will they consider the image to be sharp. In order to achieve this, one must start with a camera negative having a 4k resolution and that will, after the degradation due to the copying process, give roughly a 1.2k image on the cinema screen and this, therefore, satisfies the audience criteria.

With the DI route things are different, for as we have seen the copying process here is loss free, so it is perfectly reasonable to suppose that starting with a 2k scan, and manipulating it at this resolution, it is still easily possible to show the final scan out to film on the cinema screen with 1.2k resolution; thus, the audience should not be able to tell any difference in quality between photographic intermediates and digital intermediates.

If, at the end of the DI process, we were to show the stored digital images directly onto the cinema screen via a high-quality digital projector, it is now possible to show all of the 2k image on the screen, arguably producing a higher quality image than a film print is capable of.

The 16 mm DI route

Blowing up a 16 mm negative to a 35 mm print never looks as good as a 35 mm negative. Using the DI option it is possible to scan the 16 mm master at 2k, or even 4k resolution, though the latter will be appreciably more expensive. If you do that and write out the DI to a print, the results can be quite remarkable. This is because a 4k scan of a 16 mm master will result in at least the required 1.2k resolution on the cinema screen.

Deliverables

A considerable advantage of working with a DI is the multitude of versions that can be taken from the DI master. You can create simultaneously, or at any later date, a film copy, a digital data file that may, for instance, be delivered on a server to a cinema, a standard definition tape in any standard for transmission on television, an HD video copy, a DVD, have the ability to access the movie on the web and many more formats that exist now or may come into being in the future. Remember, the DI master will produce a picture for any screen and, as we have seen, it will more than satisfy the acutance of the human eye – quite an argument for a DI master being a reliable way to future-proof the movie.

Part Three
The Cinematographer's Craft

10
Exposure meters

Exposure meters measure brightness. Some measure the light reflected back from the scene and others measure the amount of light falling on the scene.

This chapter considers the matters to be taken into account when taking a reading and interpreting it on the meter's scales.

Camera speed

In cinematography things are mostly simpler than with still photography. You still have shutter speed and lens aperture, but your shutter speed is nearly always the same, since it is primarily dictated by the number of frames per second the camera is set to run at.

For the cinema the standard frame rate is 24 fps (frames per second) and for television we shoot, in the United Kingdom, at 25 fps. Most cameras use a 180° shutter – that is, the shutter is closed for exactly half the time and open for the other half. Some cameras can vary this, but we are not concerned with that facility at present, especially as it is rarely used. For US television 24 fps is most common, but when exceptionally high quality is required 30 fps may be used.

Shutter speed

If we are running the camera at 24 fps, which is the standard frame rate used in the cinema, and the shutter is open for only half the time, what will the exposure be? As each frame is replaced every twenty-fourth of a second and the shutter is only open to the film for half that time, then the exposure must be one forty-eighth of a second.

If we are shooting for UK television, then the same logic applies, though the frame rate here is 25 fps and, therefore, each frame takes one twenty-fifth of a second. The shutter is again open for only half the time, so the exposure will be one fiftieth of a second.

In practice, we find that some exposure meters don't have a forty-eighth of a second setting but virtually all have a fiftieth, which is fine for the television frame rate of 25 fps. For cinema, the difference is an error of 4 per cent, and that in the direction of overexposure, which is the safer direction.

Before we can discuss the different types of exposure meter, we need to know a little of how they are designed.

Average scene reflectance values

There is an international agreement as to what represents an average scene. It has been determined that the average surface of an average scene will reflect 18 per cent of the light landing on it. This is important as all exposure meters are based on this premise – they believe they are looking at something that has a reflectance value of 18 per cent. We can use this knowledge to interpret the reading that our meter is giving us.

For instance, Caucasian skin tone, the most photographed thing in the western world, is clearly reflecting more than 18 per cent – compare it with a Kodak standard 18 per cent grey card and you will see the difference. Fortunately, the difference is usually around one stop, i.e. the skin is reflecting twice as much light as the 18 per cent card, so is therefore one stop brighter. There will be occasions when we need to make this compensation – for example, when we have taken a close, reflected reading off someone's face.

Types of exposure meter

There are four basic types of exposure meter. Some work in different ways, though they have one thing in common, as we have seen – they all think they are looking at a scene with an average reflectance value of 18 per cent.

The five basic types are:

- Built-in camera meters.
- Reflected light meters.
- Incident light meters.
- Spot meters.
- A fifth type of meter, the combined meter, has recently come onto the market.

Built-in camera meters

Built-in camera meters can be very simple or quite sophisticated. The two you will come across most often in filming will be those in the Arri SR and the Aaton cameras. Both are quite sophisticated. They take a portion from the centre of the frame to be shot and give an average exposure for this portion, adding to this a smaller value for the rest of the frame. This is known as 'centre weighting' a meter, as it takes much more notice of the centre of the frame than the rest of it.

The Arri SR meter takes a small portion of the light that has been reflected onto the camera's focusing screen and sends it to the meter's sensitive cell via some fairly sophisticated optics. The Aaton takes quite a different approach in that the photosensitive cell looks directly at the emulsion in the film gate. The Aaton therefore needs to be flicked over one frame to take a reading when the camera is not running. In practice, both methods are very accurate and reliable.

These meters work very well on an average outdoor scene, especially if the camera is pointed down to exclude the sky, a reading is taken and set, and the camera is then tilted up to the original composition.

Their disadvantage is that they make no allowance for any dramatic decisions from the cinematographer, since they can only work on averages.

Reflected light meters

Reflected light meters work in a very similar way to built-in meters – in fact, they are more or less a hand-held version of the same. Being hand-held, they do give the cinematographer more control, as they can be pointed at different parts of the scene to analyse the various brightnesses within that scene.

Perhaps the most common reflected light meter is the Weston Master. This meter, with some improvements, has been around for many years. Unfortunately, even in its latest version, it is not very sensitive and can only really be used for outdoor photography. Nevertheless, as it is a classic of its kind it is worth considering.

It has a grid that may or may not cover the meter's cell, giving two brightness ranges on the meter. As you cover the cell with the grid, a new scale comes before the needle automatically, giving you the correct read-outs for the two ranges. An Invercone attachment can be added to the Weston to turn it into an incident light meter.

Reflected light meters can be pointed at an 18 per cent grey card to give an average reading of the scene and will then behave very similarly to incident light meters.

Incident light meters

As you would expect from their name, these meters measure the light incident to the scene – that is, the light falling onto the scene. They do this, in the main, by having a white dome over the meter's cell that integrates, or adds together, the light from all directions in front of the meter. This dome is usually referred to as an integrating or photo sphere. These meters are especially good for exposing reversal films. The dome does tend to collect too much light from the sky, so you will often see photographers holding their hand above the dome to shield it from this effect.

Incident light meters are also very good at measuring brightness ratios, especially those where the dome can be replaced with a flat white plate, making the meter much more directional.

An even more sophisticated integrator is the Weston Invercone attachment for the Weston meter. Here the integrator is not a simple dome but a hollow white plastic ring with a dimple in the middle. This has been very carefully designed so that there are exactly the same percentage areas of plastic facing each direction as has the human face. Thus, one gets a very accurate exposure reading for photographing a Caucasian human being. If you were foolish enough to take an Invercone apart, you would find that between its two top inner and outer surfaces there is a small piece of paper. This is in there to reduce slightly the effect of overhead light on the subsequent reading, otherwise the front of the face would be underexposed. This obviates the need to hold one's hand above the meter as one might with a simple dome attachment.

It is a very great shame that the Weston is really only sensitive enough to take exterior readings, for to be able to use an Invercone on an interior lit close-up would be very useful indeed.

Spot meters

Spot meters are a slightly different proposition in that they are not exposure meters at all, but are really brightness meters.

They work on the principle of having a lens produce an image into a viewfinder, very much like a modern single lens reflex still camera without the film body incorporated. In the viewfinder there is a small circle and the reading is taken only from within this circle. The size of the circle represents, in most meters of this type, a viewing angle of only one degree. Thus, very careful detailed measurements of scene brightness can be taken.

To make life simpler, the scale on most spot meters has a marking that corresponds to the correct reading from an 18 per cent grey card. If a reading is taken from a given part of the scene and turned into an aperture setting on the meter, then this indicated exposure will produce a density on the final print of this portion of the scene that will exactly match the density of an 18 per cent grey card. Therefore, if you are taking a reading directly from a Caucasian face, you will need to make an allowance of approximately one stop to obtain the correct density on the final print for this skin tone.

Figure 10.1 shows a scene where the white rectangle represents the view in the image of a Pentax Digital Spotmeter. At the bottom of this rectangle is a black box that contains the brightness reading from the tiny circle set on the actor's cheek; this circle is the only area over

Figure 10.1 Pentax Digital Spotmeter viewfinder

which a reading will be taken and has an angle of view of only one degree of arc. This meter makes readings in steps of one-third of a stop and the readings represent EVs (exposure values). The reading in the box therefore represents a value of eight and two-thirds; this is then easily transferred to the meter's outer scales for interpretation.

If all this sounds too complicated, don't be put off. The most valuable use of the spot meter is that, having once determined the aperture you are going to expose at, you can take readings of both the shadowed and the highlighted parts of the scene and determine if they will be within the brightness range of the film you are using. See Chapter 12 for a more detailed description of using a spot meter.

If you are using a negative stock with a range of seven stops, then as a guide you will be recording roughly three stops above the 18 per cent grey reading and four stops below that reading.

One spot meter has a further advantage. The Pentax Digital Spotmeter has an additional scale, which corresponds to the IRE (Institute of Radio Engineers of America) American television grey scale. The television system cannot handle the full seven-stop range of brightnesses our film stock can easily record – it can only handle five stops. The Pentax Digital Spotmeter shows this range on the scale nearest the operator and has the datum mark for an 18 per cent grey card clearly shown.

The combined meter

The firm Seconic has recently introduced a combined meter that, in one neat package, contains an incident meter and a spot meter. I bought one recently to use as a backup, thinking it couldn't possibly be as good as my current, separate, spot meter and incident meter. How wrong could I be! The Seconic L-508 C Zoom Master has not been out of my hand since I bought it. The meter is well thought out with logical displays and is very convenient to use. The 508's recent replacement, the Seconic L-608 C Zoom Master (see Figure 10.2), is even better,

Figure 10.2 The Seconic L-608 C meter

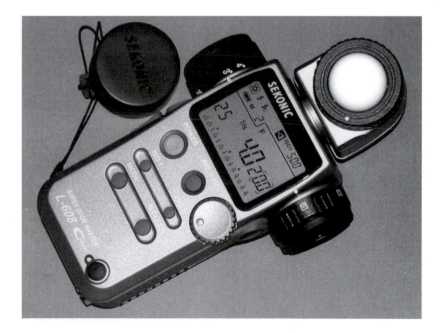

Figure 10.3 My own collection of
meters

as you don't need to choose between a meter with a still photography
or movie type scale, the new meter does both, and it also has the added
improvement of the spot meter reading showing in the viewfinder.
Remarkably, the optical path for the spot meter in these meters suffers
from no discernible flare, the bane of most spot meters, this despite
having a four-to-one zoom facility built in.

Figure 10.3 shows my own collection of meters, which are all in regu-
lar use on a daily basis. They are, from bottom left going clockwise, my
Cinemeter II, the Seconic 508 C Zoom Master, the Pentax Digital
Spotmeter and, though not strictly an exposure meter, my Minolta
Colour Temperature Meter.

11
Lighting ratios

Defining a lighting ratio

1-stop range = brightness range of 2:1

2-stop range = brightness range of 4:1

3-stop range = brightness range of 8:1

4-stop range = brightness range of 16:1

5-stop range = brightness range of 32:1

6-stop range = brightness range of 64:1

7-stop range = brightness range of 128:1

Figure 11.1 The relationship between the brightness measured in stops and the lighting ratio

A lighting ratio is the figure we give to a measured relative difference in brightness between two parts of a scene. As opening the aperture by one stop doubles the amount of light reaching the film, two surfaces where one is brighter by one stop of exposure than the other will therefore have a lighting ratio of 2:1.

Where there are several surfaces, each a stop brighter than the next, each time you open the range of your comparative readings by one stop the amount of light reaching the film will double, therefore the lighting ratio will double. Figure 11.1 shows the relationship between the difference in brightness measured in stops against the resultant lighting ratio.

Visualizing lighting ratios

It is important, before lighting a scene, to be able to visualize the lighting ratio you are going to use. It is very time-consuming to have to change your ratios after you thought you had finished lighting the set; it is unprofessional and the delay makes you unpopular with the production office.

In order to easily visualize lighting ratios, look at Figure 11.2. Here the lighting ratio between the highlight and the body of the sphere is 2:1. The ratio between sphere and shadow is again 2:1. From shadow to the deep shadow it is 4:1. The chart at the lower half of Figure 11.2 shows all the various ratios between all the parts of the sphere and its shadow.

Keep this sphere in mind and you will easily visualize all the important brightnesses on any set.

Lighting ratios for film and television

Even the finest cinema screen can only reflect a limited amount of light. In a very good cinema the difference between the darkest perceivable

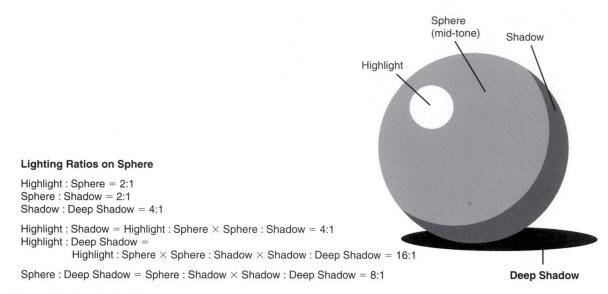

Highlight

Sphere
(mid-tone)

Shadow

Lighting Ratios on Sphere

Highlight : Sphere = 2:1
Sphere : Shadow = 2:1
Shadow : Deep Shadow = 4:1

Highlight : Shadow = Highlight : Sphere × Sphere : Shadow = 4:1
Highlight : Deep Shadow =
          Highlight : Sphere × Sphere : Shadow × Shadow : Deep Shadow = 16:1

Sphere : Deep Shadow = Sphere : Shadow × Shadow : Deep Shadow = 8:1

Deep Shadow

Figure 11.2 The relationship
between a highlight, the
mid-tones, a shadow and a
deep shadow

black and the whitest white will measure a difference of no more than
seven stops. The black will never read as absolute black, since there will
always be some spurious light, even if it is only that which has arrived as
atmospheric flare, for the highlights in the scene displayed have to travel
through the atmosphere in the cinema. The cinematographer's lot has
been much improved since smoking was banned in many cinemas.

This means that the maximum lighting ratio that we can display in
the final picture on the screen is 128:1, the equivalent of seven stops of
exposure difference. It is important to realize that any parts of the scene
outside this ratio of 128:1 will have no detail or information in them
whatsoever. They will appear as either solid black or solid white. Keeping
all the important information in a scene within the lighting ratio of the
final delivery system is therefore crucial to the success of the scene.

When shooting for television, matters are more constrained. If you
look at your television screen when it is switched off, it will appear to
be dark grey. This is as dark as it will ever get. When a picture is displayed on the television screen, parts of that picture only appear
black, or darker than the screen when switched off, because of the way
our eyes and brain expect to perceive the relative brightness between
the highlights and the shadows. A strong highlight anywhere in the
scene will make the blacks appear darker still.

Even the finest television screen can only display a brightness ratio
of 32:1 or the equivalent range of five stops of exposure range. It is
important, therefore, not to light anything in a scene that you feel the
audience should be able to perceive, even if only as a faint texture, outside a lighting ratio of 32:1. As with the cinema, but now over a much
restricted range, any part of the scene outside this range will appear as
either solid black or solid white. Parts of the scene that are solid black
or white on a television screen are far less pleasant than in the cinema,
because they attract electronic noise and, as this is an unnatural
phenomenon in normal vision, even an untrained viewer's eye and
brain will instantly know something is wrong. This must therefore be
avoided.

Figure 11.3 The range of
lighting ratios that can be
shown on different systems

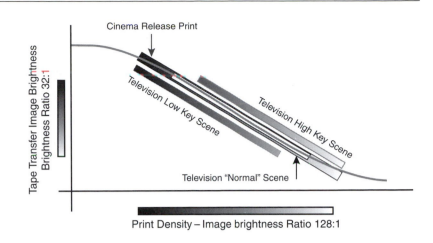

Lighting ratios when shooting for both cinema and television

The way films are funded these days, with often a significant amount of the production's capitalization coming up front from television rights and video sell-throughs, it is important that the cinematographer knows when shooting a scene exactly how it will look when delivered on the two, quite different, media. The key to this is the lighting ratio.

The first thing to realize is that the tonal range of the television version is going to have to come from within the tonal range of the cinema version. This is mainly because the television version will be, most often, telecined from the cinema print. This, in these circumstances, is not necessarily a disadvantage. You have probably put considerable effort into grading the cinema copy and, therefore, much of your grading for television, say the overall brightness and colour, will have already been achieved.

At the telecine grading of your cinema print you must remember that you don't have to take your 32:1 television version from the middle of the 128:1 cinema version. For an absolutely normal daylight scene this may well be appropriate, but for a high-key or low-key scene or a night exterior scene or snowscape it would be inappropriate.

Figure 11.3 shows the sensitometric curve for a typical cinema release print. The straight-line section has a box overlaid on it, representing the seven-stop exposure range that would result in a first-class image on the cinema screen. Inside this box is another, showing the centre section that would be used to make a normal transfer from this print to a video-tape. As is clear, the equivalent of one stop of information in the high-lights together with another stop of information in the shadows will not be transferred and will be totally lost to the television audience.

By comparing the 128:1 tonal range of the release print shown at the bottom of the print with the 32:1 tonal range of the video transfer shown at the side of Figure 11.3, you can see a very graphic demonstration of how the range is dramatically reduced.

Just below the curve is a box showing how one might transfer a low-key, or night, scene to tape. In this kind of scene it is the shadows that contain most of the information the cinematographer wishes to show the audience, so the transfer from this end of the curve only will have all the shadow detail seen when the original scene was shown in the cinema, but will have lost the equivalent of two stops of information from the highlights.

Above the curve is a further box showing the same five-stop range as the lower box, but now representing the portion of the print that you would choose to transfer if it were a high-key scene, maybe a snow or seascape. Now, of course, all the highlight information seen in the cinema is retained and the equivalent of two stops of shadow detail is lost.

It is possible, and indeed quite correct, to select any five-stop or 32:1 brightness range from the print when making a transfer to tape. Because this selection process is so important, I strongly believe all cinematographers should attend the telecine transfer of their work and should have made themselves fully conversant with the work of the telecine grader or colourist.

Using lighting ratios on the set

The most common use of lighting ratios is in the control of how we light the human face. If you have successfully lit a face and you find it particularly pleasing for the mood you are looking for, then the simplest way of noting your success, at least in part, is to record, or simply remember, the lighting ratio.

If you were lighting a rather light piece with, say, a leading lady aged perhaps late forties but playing a part written as 30 or so, a lighting ratio of 2:1 would be very flattering. This is because, with the brighter side of the face only twice the brightness of the darker side, the shadows in the smile lines by her eyes would only be half the brightness of the lit side of the face. As there would be little difference in brightness between the smooth skin and the lined skin, the lines would hardly show – all very flattering.

Using the same principle, but in reverse, your leading man in the same piece might benefit from a lighting ratio of 4:1. This would make him, certainly by comparison with his leading lady, a little more rugged than perhaps in real life, often a benefit.

Were you to be lighting a more dramatic piece, say a thriller, then you might let the lighting ratio on your leading man rise to 8:1 or three stops difference. The night scenes for the same film might rise to 16:1, but this is very dramatic – the detail in the shadowed side of the face is going to start to disappear soon and will almost certainly show as black on television.

Controlling the whole scene

As we have seen, the overall lighting ratio for a picture that is to be shown on television must be kept within 32:1, a five-stop range, and for cinema presentation it must be kept within 128:1, a seven-stop range.

The most effective way of discovering which parts of the subject will fall within the acceptable range is by measuring the brightnesses with a spot meter. A method of controlling the overall lighting ratio, and indeed controlling all the tones in the scene, is discussed in the next chapter.

12
Three-point image control

There's no such thing as exposure latitude

Many photographers refer to a particular film stock as having plenty of latitude; indeed, stock manufacturers often sell certain stocks as having great, or extended, latitude. If we are to produce the very finest images, it is important to abandon all thoughts of film having latitude and use all the tonal range of the film.

If you are using a film stock with the ability to record an image with a tonal range covering seven stops (that is, a lighting ratio of 128:1), and you knew that the image was only ever going out on television, which can only transmit a lighting ratio of 32:1, or five stops of tonal range, then you could say that you had two stops' latitude, one stop above correct exposure and one stop below perfect exposure. But why not go for a more appropriate exposure every time?

Even when shooting for television you might not want to put the five-stop range in the middle of the sensitometric curve. If you were shooting a night exterior you might wish to lay your exposure right on the bottom five stops of the full exposure range, thus taking advantage of the curved response at the bottom end on the sensitometric curve. This would be very sensible, as the non-linear response to extreme shadow detail at this point in the film's sensitivity is very akin to the human eye/brain response and can therefore, in these circumstances, look both appealing and appropriate.

The same is true of a scene containing mainly highlights, say a snowscape. Here you may decide to peg all your important tones right at the top of the sensitometric curve, thus compressing the extreme whites as they will sit on the non-linear part of the curve, where all the bright whites start to go to absolute white. This can have the effect of appearing to extend the information-recording ability of the film well into the shadows, where you may wish to show more information.

If you are shooting with a film having a seven-stop overall range and you are going to show the resultant picture in the cinema, where, as we have seen, a really good projector/screen set-up can show the full seven-stop range, then clearly you have no latitude whatsoever.

If we are to work at these extremes, or even if we wish to be certain that we are placing our chosen tones right in the middle of the straight-line section of the curve, then we will need a simple and accurate method of measuring the brightnesses in the scene and relating them to the chosen film's recording ability.

Three-point image control

To work to the accuracy required above you cannot use an incident light meter. An incident meter can make no allowance for the reflectivity of the subject behind it and that reflectivity can vary over huge margins.

A reflected light meter is required and one where the user is certain of the exact area over which the reading is being taken. Such a thing is called a spot meter. You will find a full description of a spot meter in Chapter 10.

There is a very simple way of using a spot meter to very quickly give you all the information you need for the most accurate positioning of the tones of your scene on the sensitometric curve of the film you are using. After a little experience you will not even have to think about the sensitometry at all.

Point 1

In order to establish the correct aperture to set on the lens, take a reading on the most important subject in the scene. As this will usually be your main character in the scene, then use their lit skin tone. If they are a Caucasian then the reading on your spot meter will be one stop over the setting for an 18 per cent grey card.

As we have seen, the meter expects to be pointed at something having a reflectance value of 18 per cent and Caucasian skin usually has a reflectance of around 36 per cent. This means that if the skin reads T5.6 then the lens should be set to T4. You can check this by substituting the person with an 18 per cent grey card; this will read T4. In fact, using the card is a very good way of setting this point when the person is not available. Remember, the card must be placed in the exact position of the face and should be set so that all the light that will fall on the bright side of the face falls on the card.

The only other caveat is that all the readings for this technique must be taken from in front of or very near to the lens, for only then will the reflectance of all the surfaces in the scene be the same for the spot meter as for the film.

Point 2

The second most important part of most scenes to most cinematographers is the shadows, so measuring these becomes Point 2 of the technique. We know that for cinema our tonal range goes around four stops below camera aperture; therefore, without changing any of the settings on your spot meter, look into the shadows in your scene. Four stops below the exposure we have chosen, T4, is T0.9 – therefore, any shadows that read above T0.9 will just have detail in them when shown on the cinema screen and any that read below this figure will come out as solid black.

Point 3

We know that the chosen film in this example has a tonal range of the equivalent of seven stops and therefore will record up to three stops of information above the setting for the 18 per cent grey card. As we have established that the lens is to be set at T4, then this upper cut-off point will be a reading of T11, three stops above T4.

Now explore the highlights in your scene. Any parts of the scene that read below T11 will have information in them; any that read above T11 will appear in the cinema as even, clear, white.

There is one more matter to remember when reading the highlights. When you get a reading a certain amount above the maximum recordable by the film, the image of that subject will grow, as pouring so much energy, light, into the film's emulsion causes it to disperse in various ways. Also, there is a likelihood of lens flare at these very high brightnesses. Containing this overexposure within two stops above the maximum recordable will usually prevent this happening.

Relating the three points to the sensitometric curve

Let us assume we are about to photograph an exterior scene with a 200 ISO film we have used before and we know its characteristics quite well. Experience tells us that with this film we will be able to record a seven-stop tonal range and that we will still get a little detail in the highlights if they are three stops brighter than the aperture we have set on the camera, and we still get just a little detail in the shadows when they read four stops below camera aperture.

Figure 12.1 shows a scene with the viewfinder image of a Pentax Digital Spotmeter overlaid on the scene. Let us say we were using our 200 ASA film, then the reading on the girl's face, Point 1, would be 8 in the viewfinder. Translating this on the meter's scale, this becomes T5.6. We would therefore set the lens to T4, as her skin tone will be reflecting about one stop more than an 18 per cent grey card. This means that camera aperture would now be represented by a reading of 7 in the Pentax viewfinder.

Checking the doorway to the right of the building, the shadow, and therefore Point 2, we get a reading of 4 and one dot in the viewfinder – that is, two and two-thirds stops below camera aperture and therefore one-third of a stop above black. Converting this to an exposure we get T1.0; therefore, the doorway will be just on the very edge of having information in the image and the door will, most likely, have wood grain just discernible in the image.

A reading taken on the highlight on the wall just below the dome on the top of the building is 9 and two dots in the viewfinder. As each dot in a Pentax finder represents one-third of a stop, this gives us a reading two and two-thirds stops above the camera aperture, still one-third of a stop within the three-stop limit, so there will still be a little colour and detail in these highlights – they will not have lost information or become pure white.

All the other tones

It is now possible to take readings from any or all the other tones and see exactly where they are going to sit within or outside the tonal range

Figure 12.1 How scene tones
relate to the sensitometric curve

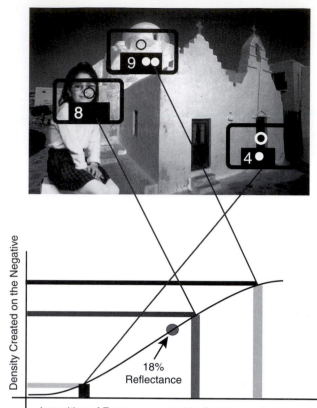

of the film. With a little practice you will be able to imagine the brightness in the final image as it relates to the nearest of the three cardinal positions you have set against the stop you have put on the lens.

Adjusting the tones

If you find that there is an important part of the scene that has read a little above the maximum white but you wish to photograph it, one relatively simple solution is to light the subject's face a little brighter. This will enable you to stop down enough to bring the highlight within the recordable tonal range. You will now need to recheck your shadows to make sure none of them have now fallen outside the film's tonal range.

More simply, if there are some shadows that fall below the recordable tonal range, then by simply adding a little more fill light you will bring them up to a recordable level. On an exterior this might simply be done with a reflector, for instance.

Control for television

Three-point image control works just as well when filming for television transmission. The only difference is that you have only two and two-thirds stops of recordable image below the reading on an 18 per cent grey card and two and one-third above. In practice, with modern film stocks, you can approximate this safely to three stops below and two stops above.

13
Using the 18 per cent grey card

The messenger

Perhaps the most important use of the grey card is as a messenger to the processing laboratory. By adjusting the brightness, and indeed the colour, of the grey card then photographing it before you shoot a scene you have, possibly, the most powerful communication tool in cinematography.

In order to use this tool you must first tell the processing laboratory you need them to participate. You can do this in three ways:

1   Before shooting, explain to the laboratory that, at the beginning of every day's rushes, there will be a grey card and would they, please, always grade the following scenes to that grey card. Tell them that when you want the grading changed you will put a new card on.
2   When the grading is to be changed, always break the roll and start a new roll. This way the laboratory grader does not have to inspect all the rushes for cards – they only need to check the beginnings of rolls. This is important, as it means the negative receives less handling and therefore has less chance of being damaged. It also saves the grader a lot of time and this encourages them to be helpful. Graders are human too.
3   At the top of the lab report sheet, always get the loader to write, very clearly, 'Grade To Grey Scales'. This is in case the grader who normally prints the rushes every night is off for some reason and the new grader does not know you are using this technique.

I have my own grey card which has printed on white Dymo labelling 'Please Grade the Following Scenes to this 18 per cent Grey Card'. When that is photographed at the front of the roll there can be very little misunderstanding as to the requirements.

Controlling print density

A technique very often used, especially when shooting a low-key scene, is to place all the important tones along the middle, straight-line section of the sensitometric curve and then have the laboratory print the scene down to its correct brightness range. The reason for doing this is to obtain a finer grain structure and dense blacks.

You get the finer grain, which in a low-key scene will show mainly in the blacks, where the grains are bigger and the exposed grains are further apart. By bringing the blacks up the curve they will be photographed on a finer-grained part of the emulsion structure.

The dense blacks come from not using the non-linear bottom end of the curve but keeping them on the straight-line section, where they are more easily and reliably controlled using the three-point system described in the previous chapter. If the laboratory printed this scene in the middle of the scale the blacks would be dark greys – just as they were exposed.

By putting a grey card on the front of the scene, overlighting it by, say, half a stop and then asking the laboratory to print to the grey card, you will be making the laboratory print all the scene down by half a stop. If half a stop is the amount the blacks were 'sat up' in the first place, then you will get back a beautifully graded low-key scene with unusually rich and dense blacks.

Figure 13.1 shows in graphical form how the darker or lighter grey card is brought back, and with it the following scene, to the correct print density.

This technique works for a low-key scene. The highlights will have been slightly crushed if both the negative and the scene have a seven-stop maximum tonal range, or a lighting ratio of 128:1. This does not usually matter as, in most low-key scenes, we are rarely interested in very much information in the highlights.

With the above example you could improve the highlights dramatically. Instead of using a negative with a finite tonal range of seven stops, why not select a negative having a longer tonal range? For example, Kodak have an excellent 320 ASA negative with a tonal range of over 10 stops; 320 ASA is an ideal speed for both night interiors and

Figure 13.1 How a laboratory corrects the exposure of an 18 per cent grey card

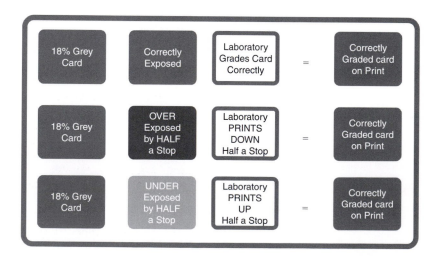

exteriors – it gives you the ability to print your work one and a half stops up or down without coming off the straight-line section of the curve.

Shifting colour

The technique described above can also be used to shift the colour balance of your final print.

Let us take an example where you wish to shoot an interior on location and there is a window in the back of the shot. Let us suppose you only have tungsten lighting with you. Also, you want to keep the scene outside the window a little bright, say one stop, and a little cool, say by the equivalent of a half blue filter, a half CTB (colour temperature blue).

The above decisions will lend a very pleasing exterior feel to the scene outside the window.

Now light the interior putting half CTB filters on your lamps. This gives you exactly the colour relationship you are looking for between the interior and the exterior. The exterior is lit by daylight, which is the equivalent of full CTB, so you have your half blue difference between interior and exterior.

Assuming that you have tungsten-balanced film in your camera, you will need to correct the film to the interior lighting, which is half blue. The filter to use would be a Wratten 85C, but this will absorb half a stop of light and you will already have lost a lot of exposure by putting the half CTB filters on your lamps.

An alternative solution is to use no filter at all on the camera to get the desired effect. To do this, put the 18 per cent grey card into the beam of one of your filtered lamps, take a reading with your spot meter from the grey card and, using this exposure on the lens, run the camera for 10 seconds. Now take a reading of the scene, put this exposure on the lens and shoot the scene.

If you tell the laboratory that you want the whole scene graded to the grey card, they will have to remove the half blue you exposed the card with and will also remove the same quantity of blue from the rest of the scene. You will now have a print that is exactly the same as had you used a Wratten 85C, but you will not have had to sacrifice the exposure loss of the filter.

The above colour correction technique works for any colour so long as there is sufficient range in the negative to accommodate the colour shift.

Intentional colour changes

If there is not sufficient range in the negative in the example above you will get crushing in the extreme tones of the colour you have shifted. This can, very occasionally, be to your advantage.

If you wish to desaturate a colour, say blue for an exterior scene, in order to create a bleak feel to the piece, then you could shoot with a short tonal range tungsten-balanced film, use no correction on the camera and correctly expose the 18 per cent grey card using the ASA rating of the film in tungsten light.

The blue layer will now have been overexposed relative to the red layer of the emulsion. This will have crushed the red highlights and lifted the blue dark tones to paler tones – this we call desaturation.

When the laboratory prints the scene correctly to your 18 per cent grey card, this will cause crushing of the highlights and lifting of the shadows in the blue layer; this will remain since we chose a film without the latitude to cope with it. The middle densities will return to the correct position on the print's sensitometric curve.

The above technique gives a very pleasing 'gritty' feel to a scene. It is much more reliable than asking the laboratory to print for the effect if they have the 18 per cent grey card to work to all the time. They will produce the same effect on each day's rushes providing you remember to put a card on before each scene and tell them that you want the following scenes graded to it.

Developments in grey cards

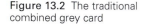

For many years, motion picture grey cards always came as a two-page card folder, as in Figure 13.2. One page has a series of progressive grey patches and the other page has a simple 18 per cent grey sheet. The custom, particularly when filming for television, was to photograph both pages simultaneously.

The grey card worked exactly as described above. The series of progressively darker grey stripes was intended to be read by the telecine operator as a stepped waveform. However, this did not really work. A piece of card, however high the quality of the printing, will only reflect from the whitest patch to the darkest patch a maximum range of four stops and that is if it is perfectly lit. Clearly, this is not even the tonal range of the television system, so does not really tell the telecine operator very much.

Figure 13.2 The traditional combined grey card

The 18 per cent grey card, on the other hand, is a universally, indeed internationally, known standard and therefore can be used as a means of communication between the cinematographer and the laboratory no matter what countries either or both are in. It therefore became the norm to photograph only the 18 per cent grey card and more or less fill the frame with it.

When filming for television it has become more and more popular to transfer the negative directly to a videotape. This is increasingly being done at the rushes stage, even on feature films, so that those rushes can be transferred directly into a non-linear computer editing system. It can also be a very high quality way of transferring a cut negative to the final, graded transmission tape.

One problem with transferring the rushes negative directly to tape, without making a print, is that the cinematographer no longer gets the grading lights that gave them an accurate guide to both the density and colour balance of the previous day's work (see Chapter 8 for a full description of grading lights).

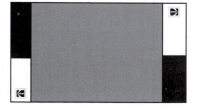

Kodak were very aware of this and have produced a very nearly ideal solution. They produced a very accurate and durable grey card (see Figure 13.3), on each side of which is a white and a black patch. Knowing that it is impossible to get pure white and black on paper they set the very dark grey, masquerading as black, and the nearly pure white paper, trying to be pure white, at very consistent densities. They called this new card the 'Grey Card Plus'.

Figure 13.3 Kodak's 'Grey Card Plus'

The next step was to produce a clever box of electronics that would recognize the signal associated with the image of this card and, if you so wished, automatically grade the following scenes to it. At the same time, the machinery will log the grading in points very similar to printer lights and can be asked to print this report to either a floppy disk or a hard-copy printer. The cinematographer can then receive a report from a direct negative-to-tape transfer, which is just as informative as they used to get from the film grader.

I have gone over to using the Kodak 18 per cent grey card, whether the laboratory I happen to be using has the electronics or not, as it is by far the most accurate and consistent card I have come across.

If you acquire a Kodak card it comes with very good instructions on the back so you can refresh your mind as to how to use it.

Conclusions

1   You can use an 18 per cent grey card to communicate your grading wishes to the film laboratory.
2   You can control both the density and colour of the print or tape transfer by using the card.
3   You must state your wish to grade to the grey card on the laboratory report sheet.
4   Talk to your laboratory before you start shooting and tell them what you intend to do.
5   It is a good idea to put a message on the card itself to reinforce the message – your laboratory will appreciate this.

14
Colour temperature

What is colour temperature?

Colour temperature is important to the cinematographer for a number of reasons. Technically, it is vital that any light source that is to appear neutral in the final rendition of the scene is emitting light of the same colour balance as that for which the film has been designed. Artistically, it is important that the cinematographer has an understanding of the psychological and emotional effects of the colour of light within a scene and that they have complete control over this colour.

In order to evaluate and control anything, we must have a unit of measurement and a means of measuring. We measure differences in colour temperature in degrees Kelvin (°K) using a colour temperature meter.

This unit of measurement is named after Lord William Thomson Kelvin, a British physicist who, at the end of the nineteenth century, developed a means of quantifying that which makes colours different. His experiment was quite simple. He took a beam of daylight coming through a hole in his shutters and caused it to pass through a simple glass prism so as to form a rainbow effect on the opposite wall. He then placed a standard mercury thermometer in the path of each separate colour and noted that the reading was very slightly different. Thus, he discovered the relationship between the colour of light and the temperature that relates to it.

Kelvin did not leave his discovery there, but went on to propose that if a black body, i.e. one having no reflective surfaces and which can therefore only emit light, is heated to a glowing state then the light coming from it will have a different colour depending on the temperature the body is heated to. The classic way to illustrate this is to imagine a poker being put into a fire. Initially, the poker is black iron, but as it warms it first glows deep red then a straw colour and as it becomes hotter still it appears white. If the fire were hot enough, say something akin to a blacksmith's furnace, then eventually the iron would appear to be blue/white.

Here we must guard against a simple confusion. At lower temperatures the colour emitted by a heated black body is red and at higher temperatures blue, but we think of red as warm and blue as cold.

Our emotional reaction to colour comes from nature, where cold days are thought of as lit by blue light, snow scenes for instance, but we react to red scenes as warm, a room lit by a log fire for instance. So, remember the actual temperature required to achieve a given colour temperature is the reverse of how we emotionally react to the colour of light emitted.

The colour temperature of a source is deemed to be the temperature of the source in degrees Celsius plus 273°C, −273°C being defined as the temperature of absolute zero. In practice, we find that there are some slight changes, some physical and some due to the source not being a black body. Therefore, a tungsten filament lamp will have a colour temperature approximately 50°K above the actual temperature of the filament.

Filters and Mired shift values

In order to change the colour, and therefore the colour temperature, of a light source we usually put a filter in its path. A blue filter will cause the light passing through it to appear more blue, but it will also reduce the intensity, or amount of energy, of the light. This is because despite, occasionally, the evidence of our eyes, filters do not add colour but can only absorb or subtract colour. A blue filter will therefore be absorbing the wavelengths of red light in order to make the subsequent light appear more blue. It does this by converting the light absorbed into heat which, as we saw earlier, has a direct relationship to light, both being a vibrational energy. It is important to remember this, as it is one reason why gelatine filters on lamps first bleach out and eventually burn through.

In order to evaluate the effect of a filter, we must have some unit with which to measure its effect. These are called Mired shift values. A Mired value is a mathematically more useful measurement for this purpose than degrees Kelvin but still represents, albeit in a different form, the colour temperature of light. A Mired shift value is therefore the shift in the colour temperature of the light passing through it that any given filter can cause to occur.

Before going any further, it should be understood that in practical cinematography one never has to calculate the mathematics – one refers to the tables or switches the colour temperature meter to give a direct read-out in shift values. The formulae are shown here as an explanation of the cause and effect of the theory.

A Mired value can be expressed in the mathematical form:

$$\text{Mired value} = \frac{1\,000\,000}{\text{Colour temperature in degrees Kelvin}}$$

A conversion table (Figure 14.1) shows at a glance the Mired values of colour temperatures from 2000 to 6900°K in steps of 100°K.

Certain filters have the ability to convert light from one colour temperature to another. The Mired shift value will be approximately the same at any given starting value. Therefore, for a given filter, the change in colour temperature caused will be more or less the same if the source of light starts at 2000 or 6000°K. This makes choosing correction filters very simple.

Figure 14.1 Mired values of colour temperature from 2000 to 6900°K

°K	0	+100	+200	+300	+400	+500	+600	+700	+800	+900
2000	500	476	455	435	417	400	385	370	357	345
3000	333	323	312	303	294	286	278	270	263	256
4000	250	244	238	233	227	222	217	213	208	204
5000	200	196	192	189	185	182	179	175	172	169
6000	167	164	161	159	156	154	152	149	147	145

Figure 14.2 Mired shift values of Wratten light-balancing or LB filters

Positive – towards yellow				**Negative – towards blue**		
Filter	**Mired shift**	**Filter factor**		**Filter**	**Mired shift**	**Filter factor**
81 –	+9	$\frac{1}{3}$		82 –	−10	$\frac{1}{3}$
81A –	+18	$\frac{1}{3}$		82A –	−21	$\frac{1}{3}$
81B –	+27	$\frac{1}{3}$		82B –	−32	$\frac{2}{3}$
81C –	+35	$\frac{1}{3}$		82C –	−45	$\frac{2}{3}$
81D –	+42	$\frac{2}{3}$		80D –	−56	$\frac{1}{3}$
81EF –	+52	$\frac{2}{3}$		80C –	−81	1
85C –	+99	$\frac{1}{3}$		80B –	−112	$1\frac{2}{3}$
85 –	+112	$\frac{2}{3}$				
85B –	+131	$\frac{2}{3}$				

Each filter can therefore be categorized as having a particular Mired shift value irrespective of the light source it is affecting.

The value of this Mired shift can be expressed as:

$$\text{Mired shift value} = \frac{10^6}{T2} - \frac{10^6}{T1}$$

where T1 represents the colour temperature of the original light source and T2 represents the colour temperature of the light after passing through the filter.

The Mired shift value can be either positive or negative. If filters deal with changes in the blue or red part of the spectrum they are called light-balancing filters (LB filters). Brown or reddish filters, shown in the left-hand column of Figure 14.2, lower colour temperature but the Mired value will, being a reciprocal function, be increased. Such filters, therefore, have a positive value. Bluish filters, shown in the right-hand column of Figure 14.2, have a negative value.

Filters that deal with green, or its complementary colour magenta, are known as colour-compensating filters (CC filters). They work in exactly the same way as light-balancing filters in that the value is always added, allowing for its mathematical sign. Figure 14.3 shows the shift and filter factors for CC filters.

Figure 14.3 Mired shift
values of Wratten colour-
compensating or CC filters

Positive – towards magenta				**Negative – towards green**		
Filter	**Value**	**Filter factor**		**Filter**	**Value**	**Filter factor**
5 M	–	+2	$\frac{1}{3}$	5 G	–	−2	$\frac{1}{3}$
10 M	–	+4	$\frac{1}{3}$	10 G	–	−4	$\frac{1}{3}$
20 M	–	+8	$\frac{1}{3}$	20 G	–	−7	$\frac{1}{3}$
30 M	–	+13	$\frac{2}{3}$	30 G	–	−10	$\frac{2}{3}$
40 M	–	+18	$\frac{2}{3}$	40 G	–	−13	$\frac{2}{3}$

Colour-compensating filters have only a limited use in cinematography, as they are primarily available for fine-tuning colours in transparency or reversal work. They do come into their own, however, when a cinematographer has to work with available light from fluorescent tubes, which often have an excess of green light. This discrepancy can be corrected by putting the appropriate magenta filter, magenta being the complementary colour to green, over the tubes or in front of the lens if no other source of light is to be added.

Filters have another important value, their filter factor. This is also shown in the tables (Figures 14.2 and 14.3). The filter factor is always expressed as the part or whole of a stop on the lens and is expressed as a fraction of a real number or a real number plus a fraction. This is the amount that the lens must be opened up to allow for the amount of light absorbed by the filter. Therefore, a filter factor of one-third will need the aperture to be opened by one-third of a stop. Similarly, a filter factor of two-thirds will need the lens aperture to be opened by two-thirds of a stop.

Here it is important to understand the difference in approach when adding together Mired shift values and filter factors. If you put two filters in front of the lens then you will combine their Mired shift values, taking regard of their mathematical sign. For example, combining two filters having shift values of +35 and −10 will result in a combined Mired shift of +25. But if their filter factors, when expressed as f-stops, were one-third and one-third, then the combined filter factor will be two-thirds and the lens must be opened up by two-thirds of a stop. Filter factors are always positive so are always added together.

In practice, it is usual to consider changes of 100°K or more as important, as this is the smallest change the eye is likely to notice unless it is possible, within the scene, to compare the sources – in which case differences down to as little as 20°K may be noticeable. This may occur, say, when a row of windows have one lamp each outside them, representing sunlight. In this case, very accurate measurement and filtration of the lamps will be required to get them all within a 20°K range.

The colour temperature meter

Colour temperature meters come in two basic forms, reading either two or three colours. The two-colour meter reads only blue and red. It is not sophisticated enough for a working cinematographer but is useful for setting filters on lamps, as this usually only concerns blue and red.

Figure 14.4 The Minolta
colour temperature meter

For the professional cinematographer the three-colour meter is
essential as it adds a reading in green. A three-colour meter is required
if readings are to be made from fluorescent tubes, mercury vapour
lamps, etc. As these, and many other sources, are frequently found on
location these days, a good three-colour meter cannot be recommended too highly.

The most popular meter in this category is the Minolta, shown in
Figure 14.4. This meter can be set to read directly in degrees Kelvin or
can have any film balance programmed into it. It can then be adjusted
to read in the Mired shift values needed to correct the light source to
the film being used. The meter will give both positive and negative
values. There is also a chart on the back of the meter very similar to
that shown in Figure 14.2 so that the equivalent Wratten filters can be
chosen without the need to make reference to any other source.

Colour film

Colour film comes from the manufacturer balanced for a given colour
temperature. That is, if the scene is illuminated with light of the same
colour temperature for which the film is balanced, then you will get an
accurate rendition of the colours in the scene.

Figure 14.5 The colour temperatures of various light sources

Daylight sources

Candle flame	1930°K
Dawn or dusk	2000°K
An hour after sunrise	3500°K
Early morning/late afternoon	4500°K
Average summer sunlight	5600°K
Sunlight from a blue/white sky	6500°K
Light summer shade	7000°K
Overcast sky	7000°K
Average summer shade	8000°K
Hazy sunlight	9000°K
Summer sky	up to 20 000°K

Artifical light

Domestic light bulb	2800°K
Photographic incandescent bulb	3200°K
Tungsten halogen bulb	3200°K
Photoflood	3400°K
3200°K +¼ blue filter	3600°K
3200°K + ½ blue filter	4100°K
3200°K + full blue filter	5650°K
HMI, CID and MSR lamps – approximately	5600°K

Normally, cinematograph film comes balanced for one of two colour temperatures: tungsten light of 3200°K or nominal daylight of 5600°K. We say nominal daylight since, as you can see from Figure 14.5, daylight comes in many colour temperatures. However, 5600°K is the international standard all daylight films are balanced for. The standard of 5600°K is used because it represents a mixture of light from blue sky with some cloud scatter.

Figure 14.5 shows the colour temperatures of a number of known light sources.

It is interesting to note that a drop of one volt in the power supply to a tungsten bulb will usually drop the colour temperature by approximately 10°K.

For the cinematographer wishing to convincingly recreate daylight, it is important to understand that the different sources – direct sun, shadow and deep shadow – will all have different colour temperatures. There are a number of reasons why the different kinds of daylight have different colour temperatures. Direct sunlight varies, mainly, due to the amount of the Earth's atmosphere it has to pass through and the amount of cloud in the sky. In the morning and afternoon the light has to pass obliquely through the atmosphere, while at noon it is taking the much shorter path directly from above. This, together with dramatically varying amounts of water suspended in the air, will clearly change the colour of the light passing through the atmosphere.

In the shadowed area, matters are different. If a reading is taken with the meter turned directly away from the sun, but still in the same place as where the sunlight reading was taken, the light reaching the meter will be that reflected off the clouds and the atmosphere itself, and this will be bluer than the direct sunlight reading. In the deep shadow, there will be no direct sunlight and all the light will be reflected – it will therefore be bluer still. This is useful in that getting those colours right can give a powerful message to the audience as to the time of day of the scene.

Figure 14.6 shows a number of readings that were taken in early August in London, when sunrise was 5.28 a.m. As you can see, the

Figure 14.6 The colour
temperature of sunlight at
different times of day

Direct sunlight	Shadow i.e. meter turned away from the sun	Deep shadow
8.30 a.m.		
4500°K	5300°K	6400°K
Noon		
5350°K	4550°K	5450°K

direct sunlight and the shadowed readings are almost transposed in the three and a half hours from morning to noon.

Correcting lamps

Correcting may not be an entirely accurate word in this context. We use it when we want to convert a tungsten lamp to daylight or a daylight lamp to tungsten. You can, of course, make partial conversions, as we shall see.

To convert a tungsten lamp to daylight you must put a full colour temperature blue (CTB) filter in front of the lamp. You will lose a considerable amount of brightness as, in effect, the lamp has become much less efficient. To convert a daylight lamp (say an HMI) to tungsten you must put a full colour temperature orange (CTO) filter in front of the lamp. Again, you will lose a considerable amount of brightness, though not quite as much as in the previous example.

To convert a daylight scene for tungsten-balanced film you put a Wratten 85 filter on the camera.

Of course, you can make partial conversions for the sake of art. For instance, if you were to film an interior that had a practical window in the shot with a daylight scene outside it and you wished the window to be just a little colder than the interior, thus heightening the feeling of separation between the interior and the exterior, then you might decide to achieve this as follows:

1 The exterior you can do little about without going to considerable trouble, so leave it as daylight, say 5600°K.
2 Light the interior with light corrected to half daylight, say 4200°K. You achieve this by using tungsten lamps with half blue filter (half CTB) or daylight lamps with half orange filter (half CTO). Which you choose matters little, it just depends which is more convenient.
3 You now have an exterior that appears colder than the interior. If you correct the camera to the interior you have achieved the objective. You do this by using tungsten-balanced film and putting on the lens a filter equivalent to a half CTO. This filter is the Wratten 85C (Mired shift value = +81).

Now camera and interior are in harmony and the exterior appears a little cool. This can be a very pleasing effect.

It has become part of the mythology of filming that, in the above example, you should use a Wratten 81EF camera filter. Please do not do this. The 81EF was designed specifically for professional Ectachrome film. It is nowhere near a half 85 and produces some very unpleasant effects when used with colour negative. One such effect is to accentuate the veins in a person's face and make them look as if they are a heavy beer-drinker. The difference between a Wratten 81EF and a Wratten 85 is a Mired shift of +60.

If you were shooting the above scene from the outside and wanted to make the interior look cosy and warm, then leave the lighting exactly as it is and correct the camera to full daylight. If you are staying with the tungsten-balanced film, then simply change the camera filter to a Wratten 85 or change the film to one already balanced for daylight. The exterior will now be colour correct and the interior will be warm and inviting.

Quarter blues (quarter CTB) are often used on backlights to increase the feeling of separation of foreground to background.

Night exteriors are often shot using tungsten film with full or half blue lamps. Full blue is often described (usually by those that don't like the effect) as American moonlight, as distinct from American night, which is what they call day-for-night in France. This comes from its perhaps being overused, to European eyes, in some American films. There is good logic behind full blue, though.

What is moonlight? It is sunlight bounced off the moon and the moon is colourless or at most pale grey. The light leaving the moon after it has been bounced off will have reduced in brightness, but it will not have had its colour temperature changed in any dramatic way. When it arrives on Earth it will still be the full blue of pure sunlight by comparison with our tungsten foreground and film.

You must make the artistic decision how blue you want your moonlight to be, but there is no getting away from it – real moonlight is roughly the same colour temperature as daylight.

15
Camera filters

We use filters in cinematography to alter the image either for technical reasons to correct the colour of the light to that required by the film we are using, or because we may wish to change the image in some way that will enhance our storytelling powers. The former is often necessary, the latter much more fun.

The majority of coloured filters are known by numbers or a combination of numbers and letters – for instance, 85 and 85B. These are simply the catalogue number they are to be found under in the Eastman Kodak Wratten Filter Catalogue. All filter manufacturers will use the Wratten filter numbers for their version of the filter in their list that conforms to the transmission characteristics of the filter in the Wratten list. A Wratten catalogue complete with transmission graphs can be an illuminating read once you know how to interpret the information.

Effects filters are usually described by some term that indicates what change they will make to the image – for example, fog filter.

Colour-compensating filters

Colour-compensating filters, or CC filters, are carefully stepped filters in the primary colours or their reciprocal colour. They are used, in front of the lens, to correct the source light to the film in use. They come in small steps so you need a lot of them to be able to cope with any situation. In reality, we rarely use CC filters in cinematography – they are mainly used in still photography to obtain an accurate original transparency, as with the reversal process there can be no correction later.

Colour-correction filters

This phrase usually refers to filters used to correct a daylight scene when shooting with tungsten-balanced film. The usual full correction filter is the Wratten 85. The various alternatives are:

Wratten 85 Full correction
         85B Full correction + slight warming – often used as standard correction when filming for telecine, as this can enhance the transfer to tape

85C   Half the correction of the straight 85 – often used
       when interior is lit to the same colour balance, so
       that any exterior, say through a window, appears
       slightly cold.

All these filters also come with a neutral density built into them. For the 85 these are available as 85BN3, 85BN6 and 85BN9. Each unit of 3 stands for a density of 0.3, which exactly halves the light passing through the filter. Therefore, an 85BN3 reduces the exposure by an extra stop in addition to the two-thirds of a stop correction needed for the straight 85. Likewise, the 85BN6 reduces the exposure by two stops and the 85BN9 by three stops, again in addition to the straight 85.

Skin tone warmer

A Tiffen 812 is very effective in warming up skin tone while having a negligible effect on the other colours in the scene. This is particularly useful for a close-up on a cold day.

Sepia, coral, colour effects, etc.

Just as you would expect from their names, these filters lend an over-all colour tint to the scene. Sepia and coral do to the film roughly what you will see in the viewfinder, but some of the more esoteric filters, say tobacco, whisky, suede, etc., can come out on film a little differently than they look to the naked eye. Coloured filters often absorb quite a lot of light to perform their trick. If you intend to use the heavier filters I strongly recommend you shoot a test under identical lighting before commencing your principal photography – this is not to say that they cannot be very effective, it is just rather surprising to find exactly what they do sometimes.

Graduated filters

Grads, as they are always known, are usually coloured or neutral density filters. They are used to colour, or darken, one part of a scene without affecting the rest of the scene.

If, for instance, you were using a neutral density grad to attenuate a sky that was too bright, then you would need a filter taller than the actual frame size so that you would have enough to slide up and down in order to place the edge of the grad accurately on the skyline. If your standard filter size was 4 in. × 4 in., then you would order your grads in 4 in. × 6 in. A 0.6 (i.e. two stops) neutral density grad is probably the most useful – I always carry one. Grads can be ordered with either a 'hard' or a 'soft' edge. I find soft-edged grads are usually the more successful. They are usually supplied where the maximum density of the filter is either 0.3, 0.6 or 0.9. The lighter one would, for instance, be referred to as a point three ND grad.

Coloured grads are used less often than simple ND grads. I carry a full set of coral grads and a few blue grads. With these I can turn almost any time of day into early morning or sunset, with both effects available in a cool or warm version. The joy of using them is that what you see in the viewfinder is near enough what you will get on film, assuming you judge the exposure correctly. If you are worried about setting the exposure, either swing the matte box away or take it off and, using a spot meter, take a reading through the filters as you have set them.

Neutral density filters

Neutral density filters are used to open up the aperture at which you will shoot the scene. This may be because you wish to reduce the depth of field for dramatic reasons or simply to improve the definition of the lens. Most cinematic lenses work best between T5.6 and T8, though these days it is nothing like as critical as it used to be if using modern lenses. The most common ND filters, as they are always referred to, are the 0.3, 0.6 and 0.9 NDs, where a density of 0.3 exactly halves the amount of light entering the lens and therefore you must open up one stop for every 0.3 of density you have added to the front of the lens.

Low contrast filters

Low contrast filters, as you would expect, reduce the overall contrast of the scene. They do this by bleeding some of the light from the highlight parts of the scene into the shadows and thus lightening them. They usually come in a set of five filters, simply marked LC1, LC2, LC3, LC4 and LC5.

The light LC filters are also useful in certain situations for creating a more flattering close-up (see the section on 'Matching shots' later in this chapter). Beware though, if you use too strong an LC filter you will get a veiling or milky look to the image.

Ultra contrast filters

Ultra contrast filters are similar to low contrast in that they will bleed highlights into shadows, but they will not cause halation or flaring around light sources or spectral highlights as will an LC filter. They also reduce the definition far less than a low contrast filter. The LC filter works with light in the image area – the ultra contrast filter works more with the incident, ambient light. They come in a range of eight filters marked ⅛, ¼, ½, 1, 2, 3, 4 and 5. They are very good at bringing up shadow detail when used with a video camera; I have achieved quite spectacular improvements to the shadows when using these filters on a Sony DVW 790 camera. The same has proved true when I have shot using HD (High Definition) with both the Sony HDW 900 and the HDW 750.

Fog filters

Fog, in reality, is caused by water droplets suspended in the atmosphere. This causes the image to be degraded more and more the further away from camera the subject is. This is simply because it has more water to penetrate. Fog filters attempt to emulate this effect.

The lighter filters reduce both contrast and definition. The heavier filters make things go rather fuzzy so do not, to my eye, reproduce the effect of nature very well.

Double fog filters

Double fogs affect flare and definition far less than standard fog filters while having a more pronounced effect on the contrast range of the image. It is claimed that objects near to the camera will appear less affected than those further away – I'm not entirely convinced.

Pro-mist filters

Clear or 'Classic' pro-mist filters give a glow or halation around intense sources of light that are in shot. They do this without reducing the contrast range as much as you might expect. Highlights become 'pearlized'.

Black pro-mists cause far less halation around highlights and produce deeper, and some say more romantic, shadow tones.

If you like their effects, then which you use is entirely a matter of taste. I much prefer 'Classic' pro-mists but I think, perhaps, I am in a minority here.

Both kinds of pro-mists are excellent on 16 mm as they do not reduce the definition as much as most of the other diffusion filters. On 35 mm the lighter grades are used to reduce what is often seen as the excessive contrast and acutance of modern film stocks and lenses. They come in a set of eight filters marked ⅛, ¼, ½, 1, 2, 3, 4 and 5.

Star filters

Beware the use of star filters – they can make things look like a poor version of a pop promo. They now come in a bewildering number of versions – Vector, Hyper, North, Hollywood, etc. Most also come in various numbers of points and widths between the lines on the filter that create the star effect.

I rarely use any but a four-point 2 mm star filter. This is the only one I carry in my own filter kit; anything else I so rarely use that I hire it in.

Star filters also add a small amount of diffusion.

Nets

Nets have different effects depending on their colour. A white net will tend to diffuse the highlights into the shadows, thus softening the contrast and making the scene higher key. Dark nets will often bleed shadows into highlights. Both will tend to take some of the colour with them. Brown nets can add a wonderful romantic look to a scene. You will need to style your lighting somewhat to suit the net you are using, especially if you have chosen a strong one.

It is not unusual for a cinematographer to put a fine net on the back of a zoom lens when shooting in 35 mm. The advantage here is that the effect remains more or less the same at all the focal lengths of the zoom, whereas in front of prime lenses the effect is different on differing focal lengths. This is mainly due to the variation in the amount of physical net in the optical path. I cannot recommend this trick for 16 mm, as the diffusion created, even with the finest net, destroys the definition of the image far more than is usually acceptable.

Be very careful that the net put in front of the lens does not become sharp enough to give you a pattern on the scene. This is a particular problem with 16 mm and short-focal-length lenses. It will become immediately apparent the moment you move the camera.

Nets will lend their own colour to a scene – a brown net will add an overall warmth and richness to the tones, for instance, the darker nets adding more to the shadows and the lighter nets to the highlights. Nets will also give a slight star effect to point sources. A candle flame shot with a black net can look very attractive and 'Christmassy'.

Matching shots

You need to be very careful when using different focal length lenses during a scene on which you are using diffusion filters. Longer focal lengths will usually need less diffusion than shorter lengths. Fortunately, these things are fairly WYSIWYG (what you see is what you get), but you have to look through with the stop on – it makes a difference.

Enhancing filters

These are very unusual filters that bring out, or accentuate, just one colour without affecting any of the others. They come in all the primary colours, though red is for some reason the most used. Both Tiffen and Hoya produce excellent enhancement filters. If you are to photograph a commercial with a red car as the product, do not leave home without a red enhancer – it will bring the car forward a treat.

Fluorescent light correction

The FLB filter corrects fluorescent light to type B film, i.e. tungsten-balanced, and FLD corrects fluorescent light to daylight film. With modern negative emulsions they are hardly necessary for cinematography, as the tubes are so much better these days and the processing laboratories have so much more experience in printing scenes shot under this lighting. Remember that if you can light all the set with fluorescent light the laboratory correction will be most successful. Mixed light is a nightmare.

Polar screens

Polar screens are used to darken the blue portion of a sky in colour photography as well as reducing unwanted reflections in particular parts of a scene. The classic use is to make the colour of a car more solid by reducing unwanted glare in the paintwork.

They are only fully effective when rotated for best effect – if the subject moves, say our car, then the effect will change as the relationship of the planes of the car change relative to both the direction of the lighting and the camera. This is also true if you pan across a blue sky – its blueness will alter depending on its relative angle to the Sun.

Polar filters reduce the exposure by one and a half to two stops. It is often best to take a reading through the polarizing filter with your exposure meter, but remember to have the filter at the same angle in front of the meter as you will place it on the camera, since the rotation of the polar filter will alter its absorption.

Filter factors

Filter factors are referred to as a simple whole number where a filter factor of 2 equals a correction of one stop of aperture. Likewise, a factor of 3 equals one and a half stops' correction and 4 equals two stops. If in any doubt, measure the filter through your meter but remember to point it at the same colour light under which you will be photographing the scene.

The pan glass or viewing glass

This is not strictly a camera filter but the piece of glass, in a holder, often worn around the DP's neck. These days it is not a pan glass at all, but its origins are so strong that the name is now synonymous with that little viewing filter and the name seems impossible to kill off. It must be said that this filter is often worn, yes by me included, as a kind of chain of office so that everyone on the set will know who is the DP.

In the days when all films were made in black and white, it was quite hard to visualize the scene before the camera, which was of course in colour, as it might be seen on a cinema screen in black and white. Early black and white film was orthochromatic (ortho = singular, chromatic = colour), meaning it was incapable of recording black and white densities as a true representation of the colour brightness. In fact, the film was sensitive mainly to blue light, which then required very peculiar make-up, ladies' faces being painted yellow and their lips black.

Black and white film stocks developed into what became known as panchromatic emulsions (pan = many). These emulsions were much more true in their rendition of colour brightness, as they could record some red and green.

Cinematographers who were used to orthochromatic film emulsions had considerable difficulty in imagining the tones that would be recorded on the new emulsions. The solution was to produce a viewing filter that the DP could look through that would, to the eye, give a fair representation of the scene as it would be recorded on the new panchromatic film. Hence the new viewing filter became known as a panchromatic viewing filter – or a pan glass.

As black and white technology progressed, various viewing filters were developed and matching pairs were sometimes available for working under daylight and tungsten light.

Nowadays, the viewing filters should strictly be called colour viewing filters, for they all try and show you the scene, not as black and white, but in colour with the tone scale modified to match the tonal scale of modern colour emulsions.

If one is honest, the most common use of a modern pan glass is to look at the clouds in the sky to see if one can get a matching lighting state from the previous shot. Many DPs still judge their lighting by them as, particularly when using a camera operator looking down the viewfinder may be inconvenient, a colour viewing filter can be a great help in judging the lighting ratio of a scene.

A good gaffer will do the sky watch for you. My gaffer has developed an uncanny ability to guess a cloud's progress across the sky. He might use his pan glass or a gaffer's viewing filter I found for him. This is incredibly dark and green, as this is the safest colour to look at the sun with, though he reluctantly admits that in the UK it's a bit too dark – hence he is always asking me when we are going to get that picture in California so that he can make proper use of the glass I gave him!

16
Depth of field

The depth of field is the distance between the nearest and the farthest subjects from the lens that will appear to look sharp. 'Appear to' is the most important part of that sentence, because in a technical sense only an image that is exactly at the distance the lens is focused at will be in focus at the film plane. *But*, when can the audience discern if an image is, to them, sharp or not?

When an image is shown on the screen, the near and far objects that appear to be in focus do so because the human eye has a limit to its resolving power. Any image we see at this resolution, or better, we will consider to be sharp. The extremes of the depth of field are the points at which the resolution of the eye has been reached.

Depth of focus

There is often confusion between the terms depth of field and depth of focus. Depth of field refers to the image in front of the lens, and may be thought of as relating to the field of view. Depth of focus refers to the elements in focus behind the lens at the plane of focus. They must not be confused.

Circles of confusion

At the moment of exposure the cinematographer or, more likely, the focus puller must be certain which parts of the scene will be sharp. We therefore need some way of measuring the sharpness of the image on the film relative to the limit of the eye's resolution at the time of viewing. Suppose an image is photographed on 35 mm film and shown in a large theatre (see Figure 16.1), and we assume our audience is one-third of the way back from the screen and we know that the eye's maximum resolving power is usually considered to be one minute of arc. We can now work out the size of the smallest dot on the screen that the eye can see in perfect focus. We can then measure the distance of our audience from the screen and, by applying a little trigonometry to this distance and our one minute of arc, come up with a physical

Figure 16.1 The resolution of the human eye

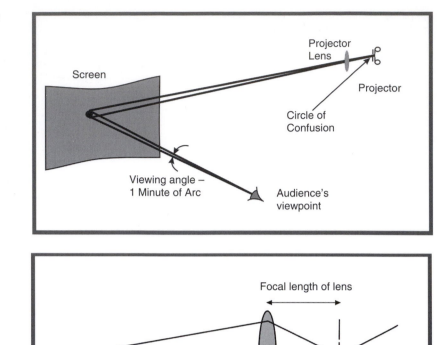

Figure 16.2 A lens focused at infinity

dimension on the screen for the largest dot that the audience will still see as a single, sharp point.

Taking the dimension of the dot on the screen and dividing it by the enlargement factor needed to bring the size of our 35 mm film up to the size of our cinema screen will find the maximum size of a dot on the film that will, on presentation to the audience, still seem to be perfectly sharp.

If you do all these sums you come up with roughly one seven-hundredth of an inch as the size of the dot on the film though, for safety, many focus pullers prefer to work from charts based on a figure of one thousandth of an inch. Then, even allowing for small errors, that which they have assumed to look sharp on the screen certainly will be.

Figure 16.2 shows a simple ray diagram where the lens is focused on infinity and therefore the distance from the centre of the lens to the plane of focus will be the focal length of the lens.

In Figure 16.3, you can see the effect of the film plane not being at the exact point of focus. You can see that the rays are covering a greater area at the film plane than at the exact point of focus. If this was the maximum dot size that we knew would look sharp to the audience, then we should be able to calculate which parts of the overall image will look sharp and which will not.

We translate depth of focus into depth of field by projecting the allowable dot size at the film plane forward to show the farthest and nearest points that will cause dots no larger than that which we have decided is acceptable.

Figure 16.3 How image size varies
at different points behind the lens

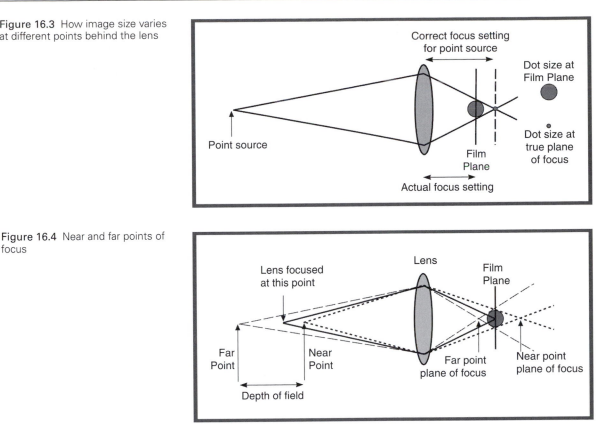

Figure 16.4 Near and far points of
focus

The ray diagram in Figure 16.4 shows that the far point creates a sharp
image behind the lens nearer to the lens than the film plane; this is shown
in heavy dotted lines. The near point correspondingly creates its image
farther away from the lens than the film plane; this is shown in light dotted lines. Absolute focus on the film plane is shown as a solid line. At the
film plane both near and far points have expanded, or become confused,
to larger dots than the original. This is the circle of confusion.

Therefore, a circle of confusion is the largest diameter of dot we can
allow a true point source to grow to on the negative and still consider
this dot to be sharp when viewed by the audience.

As a rule of thumb, the depth of focus will extend twice as far away
from the point at which the lens is focused as it will towards the lens.

Depth of field and Super 16 to 35 mm blow-ups

A precautionary note to focus pullers. There are depth of field calculators available for both 16 mm and Super 16 that are based on very
different circles of confusion. The 16 mm circle of confusion was set at
around one-thousandth of an inch. Many Super 16 depth of field
calculators work on the assumption that the allowable circle of confusion should be one two-thousandth of an inch. This is only correct if the
intention is to blow the negative up to 35 mm for showing in the cinema.

A 35 mm film, shown at any given screen size, will appear to be about
two and a half times sharper than 16 mm projected to the same size. If
we take the 35 mm circle of confusion at one seven-hundredth of an

inch and divide it by two and a half, we come to approximately one two-thousandth of an inch. Therefore, if the one two-thousandth of an inch circle of confusion on the 16 mm negative is blown up to 35 mm it will now be approximately one seven-hundredth of an inch across. In these circumstances, if the Super 16 original was shot using depth of field calculators computed at a circle of confusion of one two-thousandth of an inch, the 35 mm print should look just as sharp as if it had been originally shot on 35 mm negative. There are, of course, several other factors at play in this kind of blow-up, but at least the circle of confusion on the print will remain correct for 35 mm theatrical presentation.

Super 16 mm and 16 × 9 television

A depth of field calculator based on a circle of confusion of one thousandth of an inch has been universally used in television for shooting standard 16 mm. This works very well and produces images appreciably sharper than any television system can handle. The coming of widescreen television has added width to the television picture, with the screen height remaining the same. Nearly all film for television, at least in the UK, is now shot using Super 16, and as Super 16 has very nearly the same aspect ratio as the new 16 × 9 televisions, this negative produces almost exactly the same definition as the old standard 16 mm negative did when shown on a television with the old aspect ratio of 4 × 3.

Widescreen or 16 × 9 televisions are sold, particularly if they are capable of receiving digital transmissions, as having better definition. This is not wholly true. There are still only 625 lines being transmitted vertically, so there is no possible increase in definition there. The width is greater and to maintain the horizontal definition more horizontal bits of information are transmitted, but still only roughly the same number of bits per inch of screen width. As far as recording the image on film is concerned, the definition requirements for a standard 16 mm original shown on a 4 × 3 television and those for a Super 16 original shown on a 16 × 9 television are therefore virtually identical.

The greater apparent definition on the screen comes from less interference between the transmitting station and the receiver, and is therefore not affected by the camera origination.

Depth of field of 35 mm film when only shown on television

It is not uncommon to be asked to shoot 35 mm commercials that are only ever going to be shown on television. In these circumstances, the definition of the 35 mm film is so superior to any television system that the allowable circle of confusion may safely be reduced to one five-hundredth of an inch.

Choosing the circle of confusion to use on set

Where does this leave the focus puller and their calculations? If they are certain that the Super 16 original is never going to be blown up to 35 mm, then they would be well advised to use a depth of field calculator based on a circle of confusion of one thousandth of an inch. There is no point in working to closer tolerances, as the television system simply cannot take advantage of any greater definition. On the other hand, if there is a fair chance of the Super 16 mm negative being blown up to a 35 mm print, they should work at one two-thousandth of an inch.

Beware, though, if a calculator based on one two-thousandth of an inch is used for television production, as the focus puller will be asking the Director of Photography for around two stops' extra exposure in order to achieve the depth of field the calculator is showing as needed. This is clearly foolish, as focus pullers will be giving themselves unnecessary grief in trying to achieve the required depth and, if the DP doesn't realize the focus puller is working at too tight a tolerance and tries to light up the two stops, what would it do to the lighting budget? As a rough guide, you need twice the power to double the brightness on the set, so the DP will be asking for nearly four times the power. This is not going to be popular with the production office.

In fact, a calculator for Super 16 based on a circle of confusion of one two-thousandth of an inch will, for any given shot width, be showing exactly the same depth of field as if the shot were being taken on 35 mm. This is because, as we have seen, the purpose of the calculator is to make a blow-up to a 35 mm print that has the same circles of confusion as if the original negative had been 35 mm.

My own recommendations would be to use the following circles of confusion in the following circumstances:

35 mm film for television presentation only	1/500 in.
35 mm film for theatrical release	1/700 or 1/1000 in.
Standard 16 mm for television	1/1000 in.
Super 16 for television only	1/1000 in.
Super 16 to be blown up to 35 mm	1/2000 in.

The effect of aperture on depth of field

The depth of field obtained by any given lens is affected by two things: the circle of confusion we decide upon and the aperture set on the lens.

In Figure 16.4 we see a lens working at maximum aperture. The rays from the far point are crossing in front of the film plane and form the acceptable circle of confusion when they diverge and reach the film. The rays from the near point, on the other hand, have not yet come to exact focus at the film plane but are, again, forming a dot of the allowable circle of confusion.

If we now introduce an iris into the light path, as in Figure 16.5, this causes the rays to enter and leave the lens at much narrower angles. Drawing the rays around the same circle of confusion as in Figure 16.4, we see the near and far points of focus are now much further apart. This has the corresponding effect on the point at which the rays come together in front of the lens – they too are now much further apart – so we have created a greater depth of field.

The effect of focal length on depth of field

If one draws lines from the outer edge of the circle of confusion through the centre of the lens, the rays leaving the lens on the subject

Figure 16.5 How an iris changes
the depth of field

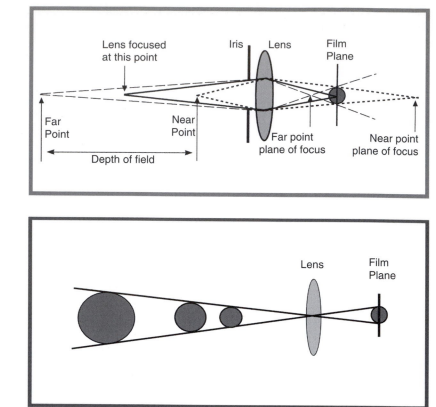

Figure 16.6 A circle of confusion
extrapolated in front of a lens

side will show the largest object, at any given distance, that we can consider will be recorded as the equivalent of a point source. Figure 16.6 illustrates this. Any rays that were to stray outside that path would create an image larger than the circle of confusion and therefore we would consider them not to be sharp.

It should be remembered that an aperture should be written down as, say, f4 or f/4. This represents a fraction, where f is the focal length of the lens and the figure underneath the bar is the aperture we are to set on the lens. This derives from the way aperture control came about. In order to control the amount of light entering the lens, and therefore the exposure, early photographers would put on a lens cap with a hole in it smaller than the diameter of the lens. They quickly realized that they needed a way of getting the same exposure on several lenses of differing focal lengths. It was discovered that if one took a figure, say 4, and divided it into the focal length of the lens and then used the result as the diameter of the hole in the lens cap of each lens, the exposure would be the same.

So, for a 100 mm lens, an aperture of 4 would need a hole 25 mm in diameter, as 100/4 = 25. To get the same exposure on a 10 mm lens, one divides 10 by 4 and uses a 2.5 mm hole.

If we consider a fairly normal motion picture lens having a focal length of 50 mm and an aperture of f2, given that we have decided on the size of our circle of confusion, we can work out the depth of field. As we have seen, the diameter of the lens, or its stop, will be 50/2 = 25 mm.

Figure 16.7 represents such a 50 mm f2 lens. The short dotted lines represent the rays that will cross between the film plane and the lens and go out to form the farthest point of the depth of field. Objects only

Figure 16.7 Depth of field for a
given circle of confusion

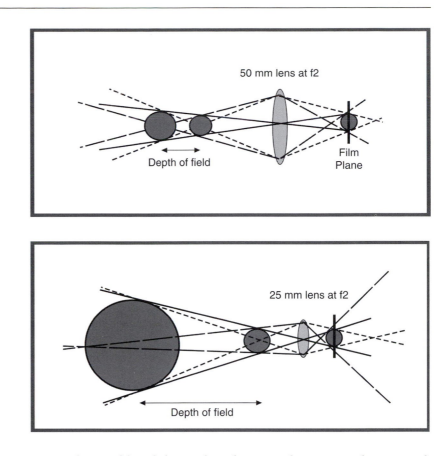

start to be considered sharp when these rays have come close enough together to be inside the hard lines.

The rays that will form the near point cross over inside all the other lines beyond the lens, and it is only when they diverge and cross the hard lines that they cease to be sharp, having formed the far point of focus at the crossing point.

Figure 16.8 has been drawn in the same proportions as Figure 16.7, but represents a 25 mm f2 lens. Two things change as a result of this new lens: the film plane halves its distance from the centre of the lens and the diameter of the lens is smaller. The ray diagram is drawn with exactly the same parameters as Figure 16.7, but due to the new proportions of the lens the rays forming the far point cross the hard lines much nearer the lens and the rays forming the near point do not diverge and cross the hard lines until much further away. Thus, a much greater depth of field is created.

The mathematics of depth of field

It is never necessary to go back to first principles and do the mathematics involved on the set. Commercially available calculators are very reliable and are to be trusted.

Before displaying the mathematics involved in computing the depth of field in any given situation, the idea of hyperfocal distance must be understood. Knowing the hyperfocal distance can be useful in practice, for it tells us the maximum depth of field starting with infinity and coming back

Figure 16.8 How focal length
affects depth of field

to the camera. If a lens is set at its hyperfocal distance, the depth of field will be from infinity back to half the value of the hyperfocal distance. This can be useful if a camera is to be run unattended, for a stunt perhaps.

The formula for obtaining the hyperfocal distance is:

$$\text{Hyperfocal distance} = \frac{(\text{Focal length of the lens})^2}{\text{f-number} \times \text{Circle of confusion}}$$

Of course, all the dimensions have to be in the same form, inches or millimetres.

Having calculated the hyperfocal distance, it is possible to compute the near and far points of the depth of field. One needs two computations, which are:

$$\text{Camera to nearest limit} = \frac{H \times S}{H + (S - F)}$$

$$\text{Camera to farthest limit} = \frac{H \times S}{H - (S - F)}$$

where:
H = Hyperfocal distance
S = Distance from camera to subject
F = Focal length of the lens.

Depth of field calculators

Look-up tables

Depth of field calculators come in three main types. You can use look-up tables as found in many books on the more technical side of cinematography and as supplied by many lens manufacturers. These are accurate but are limited in their variations, for each page only refers to one lens and each line only refers to one subject distance; therefore, they are rather inconvenient to use.

Rotary calculators

The original rotary slide rule for the calculation of depth of field was the 'Kelly', so called for it was created by a British cameraman by the name of Skeets Kelly. The original version was purely for shooting 35 mm in the Academy aspect ratio. It came out shortly after the Second World War. This rotary calculator has, in the intervening years, gone through many incarnations and is currently produced by the Guild of British Camera Technicians (GBCT). Figure 16.9 shows a 16 mm imperial Guild calculator. It is available for both 16 mm and 35 mm lenses in both imperial and metric distances. On the back of each depth of field calculator are a myriad of other calculations you may need on the set, such as exposure time to shutter angle ratios, etc., as shown in Figure 16.10. There is even an HD (High Definition) version available, though as most HD cameras don't have variable shutters, this calculator has metric values on one side and imperial on the other.

Most focus pullers, AC2s, still refer to the calculators of this kind as their 'Kelly', though younger ones are beginning to use the phrase

Figure 16.9 The GBCT rotary 'Kelly' depth of field calculator

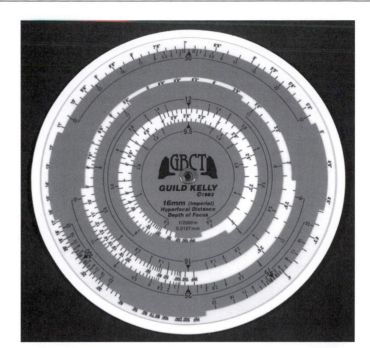

Figure 16.10 The reverse side of the Guild or 'Kelly' calculator, which enables many useful calculations to be done at speed

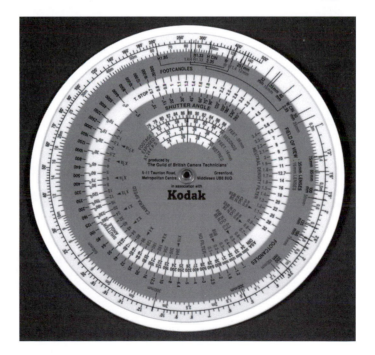

'the Guild calculator'. If I may make a small private request, may we always use the phrase Kelly calculator, for without Skeets we would not have this very useful tool and I think he should be remembered for his contribution to keeping focus pullers sane. I was introduced to Skeets by my father and he was a delightful man – another good reason for keeping it known as the Kelly calculator.

Samuelson calculators

There have been several generations of the Samuelson calculator, the latest of which is shown in Figure 16.11. They are more versatile now in that they will allow calculations using a variety of circles of confusion, and the use of both a rotating and a sliding scale are of great value when working with a zoom lens, as an infinite amount of focal lengths can be chosen.

Initially, the Samuelson calculator looks complicated, but I know focus pullers who are experienced with it to be very fast and accurate. It is a calculator very much worth considering, as the single unit will work for all lens lengths, all circles of confusion and virtually all image formats.

Digital calculators

A more recent development is the ability to do your depth of field calculations on a palmtop calculator. My favourite is the pCAM depth of field calculator, together with the sophisticated general information program pCINE. Both these programs work on most Palm-based

Figure 16.11 The Samuelson Mk. III depth of field calculator

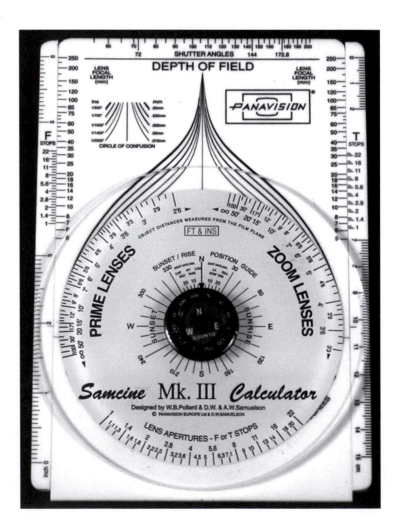

hand-held computers, they are incredibly fast and, in my experience, very reliable. Figure 16.12 shows the screen on my Palm m500 calculating the depth of field for a 25 mm lens shooting 35 mm 1:1.85 aspect ratio assuming a circle of confusion of one-thousandth of an inch or 25.4 microns. It shows all will *appear* sharp from 7 ft 7 in. to 29 ft 4 in. with the lens focus set at 12 feet. It took this program less than a blink of an eye to do this calculation.

I have recommended this depth of field calculator to many of my students and quite a number of my crews, and almost all of them have adopted it.

You can download these programs from the Internet. They were developed by an AC1, David Eubank, in association with Suharto Iskandare, and can be found at www.davideubank.com. You can download it for free, but as both programs cost only a few dollars I would entreat you to pay for them – they are exceptionally good value.

Figure 16.12 A Palm Pilot showing a pCAM screen

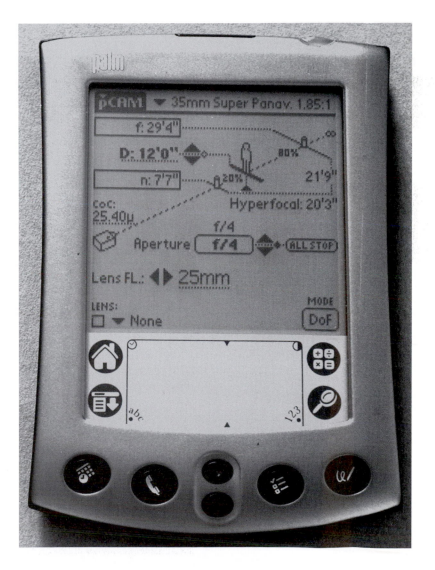

17
Testing

Why so much checking?

There are two reasons for meticulous preparation of all the equipment and stores you will need for a shoot.

The first is clearly your own professional pride and the need to pack equipment in such a way that the crew can find any piece of equipment quickly and efficiently, even in the dark of a night shoot. Also, it is essential that all the equipment starts the job in the finest possible condition.

The second reason, and indeed the reason for some of the more obscure test procedures, is that the production company probably raised a completion bond to insure the picture gets finished and the bond company will require hard evidence that all was well before you started.

A completion bond is a form of insurance taken out by the production company in order that they, the production company, will be reimbursed any expenses incurred due to unforeseen circumstances. For instance, an artist might become ill during production and delay shooting for several days. The completion bond company will then be responsible for all additional expenses incurred.

Another example might be several rolls of film being found to be scratched after development. The bond company might have to pay for a reshoot. It is clearly in everyone's interest to be able to prove that none of the camera bodies nor any of the camera magazines were scratched when first loaded onto the camera car at the beginning of shooting.

For these reasons everything, but everything, must be checked and, where possible, physical proof of a successful check must be available.

Who checks?

The focus puller is normally in charge of the preparation and will almost always be assisted throughout by the clapper loader. This is sensible, for during the shoot the focus puller will be responsible for the day-to-day running of the camera and the loader will be expected to know exactly where every single piece of equipment is at any given time.

If there is more than one camera crew on a shoot, each crew will usually be responsible for, and prepare, their own equipment. Occasionally, on very big shoots with multiple cameras, I will nominate a head focus puller and head loader. This does not denote seniority but is necessary so that any problems with any of the crews' equipment comes through them to me, the DP. This is important as my responsibility is to the director and for the photography, and if all the crews came to me directly it may simply take too much of my time.

Even on a short television shoot a minimum of three days should be allowed for testing. This is a continual bone of contention with the production office, who frequently profess to see no reason why it can possibly take more than a day and see no reason to find all involved three days' pay. The reason for three days is simple. The first day will be very busy and long, as all the testing requiring film to be run through the camera must be done on this day. All other matters are put aside.

The following day should, unless the shot tests show major or multiple problems, be easier. The morning of this second day is put aside for the careful inspection of the test rushes. These may be seen at the hire house where testing is normally carried out or you may have to go to the laboratory to find adequate projection facilities. It is essential that the projector and screen used for viewing the tests are of the highest quality. I have known occasions where faults have been seen, a huge amount of work put into correcting them, and they have eventually turned out to be a projector fault. It is also desirable that the projector used for this viewing has an oversized gate, so that the edges of the frame are visible on the screen; these are rarely found anywhere but hire houses and laboratories.

The third day of testing is required because this world is not perfect and it is very rare for there not to be at least one piece of equipment, and there will often be more than one, that is not up to your standards. This will need maintenance or replacement and will then require a further film test. This test will be shot on the afternoon of the second day and viewed on the morning of the third day. If things are still not satisfactory you are in trouble and somebody may then have to have strong words with the hire house.

Tests that involve shooting film

Tests that involve shooting film include:

- Camera steady tests
- The frame leader
- Scratch tests
- Fog tests.

Camera steady tests

Every camera body you are likely to use on the shoot must have a test run on it to check that the camera mechanism is registering the film in the camera gate with an accuracy at least as good as the manufacturer's specification. This is called the steady test. Many hire houses will set their own standard a little above the manufacturer's; if they do, then work to this standard.

Steady testing involves running the film through the camera twice. On each occasion a slightly different image is recorded. The type of images used vary, but all have in common the idea that the two images can easily be seen to move, one against the other, and many of the steady testing methods give some measurable indication of how much the two images move relative to one other. It is important to realize that it is likely that a very small amount of relative movement between the two images will be seen. What is important is to check that the amount of movement has fallen within the acceptable tolerances.

Before the first exposure of the steady test you remove the lens from the camera and, after opening the shutter, mark a small cross on the film emulsion. The lens is replaced and the first exposure made. In order to rewind the film for the second exposure it is necessary, with most cameras, to have a darkroom available that is fitted with a rewind bench. Most of the hire houses have these. Be very cautious of running the film backwards through the camera as this may, in itself, damage the perforations and lead to some unsteadiness between the exposures.

After being rewound, the film is relaced in the camera mechanism and the camera inched over until the cross you made is back in the gate. With 35 mm cameras it is wise to put a line close to the top and bottom of the gate so as to ensure you are engaging with the same set of perforations. With 16 mm, where there is only one perforation per frame, this is not a problem. Be very careful when marking the film not to damage the camera gate in any way.

The frame leader

Another test that will be required by the completion bond company, and very probably by the camera operator, will be the shooting of a frame leader. This involves looking through the viewfinder with the camera at perfect right angles to a wall and with the lens focused on it. Small coloured arrows made from camera tape are then stuck to the wall pointing to the exact position of the corner of all the aspect ratios the film may be shown in.

Figure 17.1 shows how the frame leader should look on the wall. This illustration shows a frame leader drawn from a 35 mm camera's

Figure 17.1 A frame leader

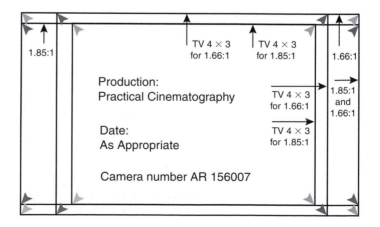

viewfinder where the outer frame has an aspect ratio of 1.66:1, which will represent the camera gate and, as this can be varied on most 35 mm cameras, is known as the 'hard mask'. The next set of markings are only different in being slightly shorter in height and represent an aspect ratio of 1.85:1. This is the aspect ratio used in most European cinemas. Finally, the much squarer rectangle shows the portion of the frame that will be used for a transfer to tape for television.

The purpose of shooting a frame leader is to reassure both the completion bond company and the camera operator that the aspect ratio markings in the viewfinder correspond exactly to the negative aperture of the camera gate. This is best done by viewing the negative. Some operators will ask for a length of frame leader to be sent to the laboratory in order that a short length is printed before each day's rushes or dailies.

The frame leader must be clearly marked with the production name, the date and the camera identification. This way, there can be no confusion as to which camera and viewfinder markings it refers to. This is not just essential when there are several camera bodies on the shoot, for it is surprising how often one laboratory will have several tests going through the bath on any given night. This also applies to hire houses who may have several productions testing at once.

This test is not ideally viewed on a projector, but with a low-powered microscope. As I have said, most projectors do not show the full camera aperture unless they are at the laboratory or hire house, where an oversize gate can often be found; even so, microscopic investigation will often be more critical than projection.

There is a further use to which the frame leader can be put. If the rushes are being transferred to tape, it is not uncommon for the rushed telecine to slightly underscan the picture. This produces a tighter composition than the operator originally framed for. If this is suspected, then a length of frame leader can be sent through with the next batch of rushes and all will be revealed. This needs doing disappointingly often. Just as when rushes are to be provided as a film print, some operators will ask for a length of frame leader to be sent to the transfer house making the tape copies in order that a short length is transferred before each day's rushes. This usually overcomes the problem of the telecine underscanning.

Scratch tests

Every camera magazine must be tested for scratching. This is done by running 20 feet or so of film through the camera using each and every magazine. This simultaneously scratch tests the camera bodies. The film need not be sent to the laboratory – simply unwind the last three or four feet of film from the take-up side of the magazine and inspect both sides of the film through a strong magnifying glass.

A trick many loaders use is to 'catch the light' on the film when looking for scratches. When this is done the surface of the film will shine and any scratches will show up as black lines.

If the film shows short scratches identical on every frame, then as likely as not either this has occurred in the camera gate or the loop of film just before or just after the gate has been too big and has rubbed on the camera body at the moment the loop has been at its largest.

If a scratch shows as a continuous line, then there is probably something stuck in the light trap of the magazine or possibly one of the lay-on rollers in the magazine is not rotating freely. If the magazine employs felt rollers as part of the light trap, they may need cleaning.

If you are in any doubt as to where the scratching is occurring, run a second test and before you remove the film from the camera take the lens out and mark the frame in the gate. Now, when you unload the film you can count the number of frames before or after the gate to the point where the scratch starts. If you now mark this point and reload the camera again with the original marked frame in the gate, your new mark will be exactly where the scratching is occurring.

You will need to check with the completion bond company as to whether they wish to hold a developed copy of your scratch tests. If they do, only shoot them after you are confident your eyeball tests are absolutely free of scratches and do not run the negative you will be sending them through a projector, where further scratching may occur. Simply run an eyeball test on the processed negative to reassure yourself all is well.

Fog tests

These are rarely carried out unless you are going to a very hot and sunny country. Point the camera at a wall and write on the wall the magazine number, then underexpose this by at least one stop to give a dark grey image on which to look for fogging. Get a strong lamp and run 20 feet of stock through each magazine while hand-holding the lamp and pointing its beam at all the joins between the magazine door and its casing, then do the same for the camera door. On projecting the print you will quickly see whether any light is getting through the seals.

With a fog test it is useful to light the room and the magazine number on the wall with a different coloured light than is hand-held around the camera and magazine. So if the room and wall are lit by tungsten light, use an HMI daylight lamp for the test. Conversely, if the room and wall are lit with daylight, use a tungsten lamp for the test. This way even the slightest light leakage can be detected as it will show up as a different colour to the image on the screen.

Lens testing

All the lenses should have been collimated by the hire house before delivery to you for testing. Should your DP be supplying some or all of the lenses, then most hire houses will check their collimation free of charge. Any faults found should be put right before your testing period starts.

The lens tests that must be carried out are:

- Infinity test
- Resolution test
- Focus tests at various distances.

In addition, as many focus pullers do not trust the engraved scale on some lenses, they insist on marking up critical focus points on plastic tape applied around the lens barrel. They will also mark up individual focus rings if they are using something like the Arri follow-focus device. If this is to be done, then both left-hand and right-hand rings need to be prepared.

Infinity test

It is important that all your lenses can focus as far as infinity. To test this can be taxing as, other than with the iris wide open, there will be sufficient depth of field for almost any lens to show infinity as sharp. There is a difference of opinion on this test. Some focus pullers insist on shooting this test, while others feel it is sufficient to eye-test the lenses. My feeling is that an eye test is probably adequate. If you decide to shoot a test then you have two options. If the camera you are using has a variable shutter, then you can close this down to obtain the correct exposure with the lens wide open. If the camera does not have a variable shutter, then you will have to shoot at dusk or dawn.

You must not, under any circumstances, put neutral density filters in front of the lens for this test. Putting glass filters in front of a lens will alter the point at which the lens focuses on infinity. This is particularly noticeable with lenses of long focal length. Indeed, it is essential that all the longer lenses are infinity tested with and without a Wratten 85 filter to check they can reach infinity in both conditions. If the DP you are working with tends to use a lot of filters, then test the longer lenses with several filters on.

You will notice that with most long-focus lenses the focus barrel will go past infinity. This is to ensure that you can reach infinity with several filters in front of the lens, as the effect on infinity when adding extra glass to the front of the lens is greater the longer the focal length of the lens.

Resolution test

There are a number of wall charts available for lens testing and most of them employ a series of parallel white lines on a black surface. The lines are so arranged in blocks of finer and finer lines in order to discover how fine the line must be before the lines cannot be seen apart. This is the limit of the lens's resolution. These measurements only work if the chart exactly fills the frame. A good example of such a lens test chart, designed and produced by KJM Consultants for Panavision, can be seen in Figure 17.2. Do not copy and use this illustration from the book – if reproduced in this way it will not have sufficiently fine definition to give any meaningful results.

These days it is more common to test the finite resolution of a lens on the bench either by measuring its MTF (modular transfer function) or by projecting a very accurate chart, similar in appearance to that described above, through the lens onto a wall where, due to the large size of the projected image, the judgement of which are the finest lines resolved can more easily be made.

The testing of the ultimate resolving power of a lens is best done in conjunction with the specialist at your hire house. If you have worked with the hire house before and trust them, then you can, quite reasonably, ask them to have checked all the lenses before you start your testing.

Figure 17.2 A lens test chart

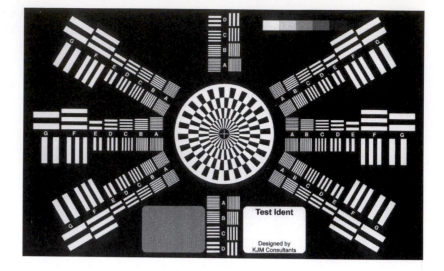

Figure 17.2 A lens test chart

Focus tests at various distances

Focus testing is time-consuming and must be done with great care. It usually involves covering a wall of the test room with lens test charts, such as that shown in Figure 17.2. This is so that the entire frame can be filled with charts. An alternative, but more time-consuming, method is to relocate a chart at the top and bottom edges of the frame, both sides and all four corners. This is in addition to keeping one at the centre. Mercifully, most hire houses have a wall of charts, or something similar, already set up, but moving charts around is cheaper if you are having to test independently.

As previously stated, a lens test chart can only be used for measurement of resolution when it exactly fills the frame. With focus testing, we are not looking for a measurement but are checking if the lens focuses at the distance indicated on the lens barrel or, if it doesn't, making a new mark at that focus ourselves; secondly, we are checking if the lens maintains the focus at the edges of the frame when it has been focused at the middle of the frame.

For focus testing you are only using lens test charts as very easily readable images from which to tell if the lens is focusing properly.

Each focus puller will have a preferred set of distances at which they like to test and mark up the lenses. They may not always use the same ones. For example, if you are about to shoot an intimate script, and are on location, then the nearer focus points are more important, since that is where your cast are going to be most of the time. On the other hand, if you are going to shoot a western, you are going to spend some of the time shooting close-ups but a lot of the shoot will be nearer infinity.

Many focus pullers simply abandon the distances engraved on the lens and mark up their own with thin tape and a fine, waterproof marker pen.

The technique is to set up the camera exactly at right angles to the wall of test images and perfectly central to them. Every lens must then be checked, through the viewfinder, at every distance the focus puller requires. This does take a long time, but can save much grief on the set during shooting. Some film must be exposed with each lens at each position. Ideally, two exposures should be made, one at the maximum aperture of the individual lens and another at a stop the DP nominates as one they will be using a lot.

Do make sure that the lens flange to film plane depth and the lens flange to viewing screen distance have been checked to the highest possible standards available by the camera supplier before you carry out the focus tests, otherwise you are wasting your time.

Gamma testing

The last test that requires film to be sent to the laboratory is the gamma test. This requires you to remove 30–50 feet of film from a roll of every type and batch of film you will be using during production. When asked to carry out a gamma test the laboratory will make an exposure on each sample using a sensitometer: they will process the film and, using a densitometer, will read off the sensitometric curve for all three colour layers of the negative. They will send back the test negatives together with graphs of the sensitometric curves.

As reading these graphs takes experience and specialist knowledge, it is quite reasonable to phone the laboratory and ask them if the tests were satisfactory. If you wish to be doubly safe, ask them to fax the production office with their opinion.

What to do with the film tests

Having successfully completed all the film tests described above, they should all be gathered together and carefully labelled. Most usually they will then be lodged with the cutting room, assuming the editor has started at the beginning of shooting. Occasionally, they may be sent to the production office or the completion bond company. Ask the production office which they prefer.

Non-film testing

There are a number of non-film tests that it is prudent to carry out:

- Batteries
- Tripods
- Heads.

Batteries

It is sensible to fully charge all your batteries as soon as possible and leave them untouched during your testing days. Check them at the end of your testing period – they should all have held a full charge over several days; any that have not should be changed.

Tripods

This may be done by the dolly grip, but all the tripod legs should be tested to make sure they are in good condition and that they lock properly. This may seem obvious, but on a recent shoot a tripod leg gave way and deposited a quarter of a million pounds worth of camera and lens assembly rather dramatically on the studio floor – an embarrassment one would wish to prevent at all cost.

Heads

Every tripod head should be checked. Geared heads need skilled adjustment and many operators will want to check them themselves. Some operators provide their own heads. If this is the case, then it can safely be assumed that they will bring them to the set in perfect condition.

Fluid heads should be checked for smooth movement over the whole of their range and on every friction setting. It is also wise to set them up on the first day of testing and just leave them standing to check for any fluid leaks.

Remote heads can be a problem as they often arrive with a crane on the day they are going to be used and therefore you have no chance to test them. Fortunately, the crane and head should come with a skilled, specialist operator and all will be well. If you are having a remote head from the start of production, make sure whoever is going to operate it is happy with its performance.

Stores, supplies and expendables

Ordering expendable stores before starting production can be a touchy business – great care should be exercised. Some production offices are unaware of the quantity of consumables that will be used on a large production. Some have, sadly, been persuaded to purchase far more than could possibly have been needed and know full well that the over-ordering was used to stock personal supplies. As you are going to be working with the production office for the duration of the shoot, it is as well to get off to a good working relationship. Therefore, order your stores, supplies and expendables with care.

On a long production it is wise to order only the amount of stores etc. you will need to get halfway through the schedule. You can make this clear to the production office, thus making them aware that you will only reorder as needs be. My crews have, in the past, found this a good and reliable strategy.

Many hire houses have in-house shops or store rooms and are only too happy to supply most of your needs on site. They are often good value but do check, as overcharging annoys the office as much as over-ordering.

Your report sheet books and can labels should be obtained from the laboratory you intend to use. As the layout will be familiar to them, this reduces the possibility of any misunderstanding. The laboratory can, as often as not, supply you with spare film tins. Extra film bags should be purchased new – only the bag the film came in from the manufacturer should ever have a roll of rushes put back into it. Never use a bag that has previously been used by someone else – you have no idea what dirt and dust it may contain. Film cores can also usually be obtained from the laboratory; if not, then try the stock supplier or your hire house.

I know a loader who has designed a report sheet blank on his laptop computer. During the day he fills in the sheet as he goes along and prints it out at the end of the day. This is very impressive, but does lack the familiarity aspect of the laboratory's own report sheet. Perhaps if this appeals to you a good idea may be to send a blank copy to the laboratory contact for approval. They will probably be quite happy with this and it will overcome the familiarity problem, as well as starting a good working relationship with the laboratory.

If you use computers for any purpose when filming, always back your work up regularly and keep the backup in a separate place from the computer. Computers are replaceable and should be insured, but the greatest value is often the information they contain and this can be irreplaceable. If you are going to have your computer with you on a regular basis, it might be a good idea to ask the production office to add it to the company's insurance list.

The all-important 18 per cent grey cards can be obtained from the laboratory, Kodak or several independent suppliers. I get mine directly from Kodak, put my message on them as I have described and bring my own to the set. My regular loaders now order them for me and present them to me on the first day of shooting already labelled. Whatever cards you order, check with the DP first to find out their preference.

The current trend for clapperboards is to use what have become known as 'backlight boards'; the layout of a typical backlight board is shown in Figure 17.3. These have the clap sticks still made out of wood, but the board is made from white, translucent Perspex or Plexiglas. The idea is that they should be just as effective when lit from the front as from the back, which indeed they are. Temporary marks on the board, such as slate numbers, are made with a dry marker pen and can therefore be easily rubbed off. I very much favour them, as anything that makes the board easier for the cutting room to read must be a good thing.

Figure 17.3 The backlight clapperboard

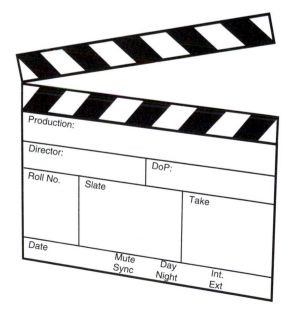

If the production is sufficiently well funded and is to shoot for a reasonable time, then it is worth having the backlight board engraved with all the permanent information. If not, put waterproof adhesive tape on the board first, mark the information with a waterproof marker and then cover with a further layer of waterproof tape. This makes for an easily readable board, the backlight idea still works and the whole lot can be peeled off at the end of the production.

One thing I do not approve of, and most of the backlight boards suffer from it, is the marking of the lines on the clap sticks with the upper and lower lines going in the same direction. They should go in the opposite directions, as in a chevron, as this makes it much easier for whoever is synching up the rushes to see the exact moment the two sticks come together.

The camera car

Calling it a camera car is a hangover from the past as nowadays it is, as often as not, a three-ton truck! Ideally, the sides of the truck should have shelving with a large lip or bar at the front so that cases of equipment can travel in complete safety. A bench is essential for assembling the camera.

Some trucks come with a small darkroom in one corner. This looks to be a good idea but it is essential that the loader checks that the darkroom is totally lightproof. This can be a time-consuming and unpleasant exercise, as one only acquires full night vision after 20 minutes, and 20 minutes in a small, dark and airless room can be a taxing affair even if you have taken your MP3 player with you.

Distrust of camera car darkrooms has led several loaders I know to prefer a second bench on which they can leave their Harrison changing tent permanently set up. If a darkroom is still fitted it usually becomes a store for consumables so as not to waste space.

If you are filming in the height of summer or in hot climates, a small fridge for the day's film stock is a good idea. Clearly, it will need plugging in to a power supply, but a friendly word with the gaffer will usually ensure one awaits you on arrival at every location. It is surprising how long a fridge will stay adequately cool when switched off providing the door is never opened. See Chapter 6 for guidance as to storing film stock at different temperatures.

Once the habit of supplying power to the camera car has been established, a kettle and a coffee machine are a good idea, especially on cold night shoots. Make sure the fridge has sufficient space for all the film stock – in hot countries it is not uncommon for cans of coke and beer to mysteriously find their way into the fridge. Before letting any drinks into the fridge, do check if you are on an alcohol-free production; if you are, then be rigorous about not letting your fridge get so contaminated, as I can envisage a situation where the loader in charge of the fridge could get fired when, unknown to them, some friendly person has stocked up.

Offering refreshment to the lighting and grip crew usually ensures adequate power supplies, though I must admit to being lucky in this respect, as my regular lighting crew insist on taking over the coffee and tea duties and have even presented me with a thermally insulated mug with their nickname for me engraved on it – that's service!

Part Four
Operating

18

Composition and the rule of thirds

Framing using the rule of thirds

Perhaps the most used and useful rule of composition is the rule of thirds. It is really very simple. If you imagine a frame with a line across both the horizontal and the vertical positions, one-third of the frame width in from each of the four edges of the frame, then any object placed on this line will have added importance in the overall picture. This division also produces nine identical boxes within the frame; later we will explore the importance of this.

Figure 18.1 shows a 16×9 frame with all four of the third lines shown. As you will appreciate, not only do the third lines have importance, but the position where they cross each other becomes a position of even greater importance within the overall frame as it acquires stature from both the horizontal and the vertical third lines.

Let us explore how this might work in practice. If we were to photograph a cityscape, say across a lake, we might choose to frame for the skyline – this, after all, would be the obvious choice. If so, the shot might look like Figure 18.2.

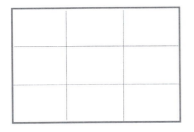

Figure 18.1 A frame divided into its thirds

Figure 18.2 A horizon set on the lower third

Figure 18.3 A horizon set on the upper third

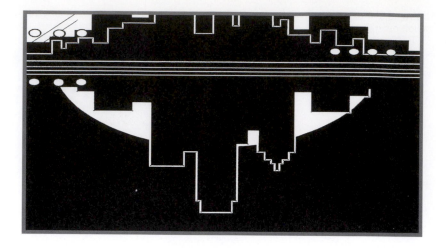

Figure 18.4 Central composition

Here the horizon is set on the lower third and produces a very pleasing composition, clearly at dusk.

Figure 18.3 is exactly the same view but now composed very firmly with the horizon on the top third. Many things have changed as a result of this compositional decision. Perhaps the most striking thing is that the scene now appears to be night. Simply by choosing to make the reflection in the lake the dominant part of the scene we have significantly altered the audience's opinion of the scene. In addition, we have started to talk about very different matters with regard to the script. For instance, Figure 18.2 might be about the financial district of the city, but Figure 18.3 could be about the demise of its fishing fleet. To use the shots in the reverse context would be nonsensical. Such is the power of the compositional choices.

Now let us bring in two more ideas – composing on the left and right thirds and introducing movement into the frame.

In Figure 18.4 the dancers are in the middle of the frame – this is usually a boring position, but the clear movement of the subjects can make it very exciting. The effect of the shapes within the frame is so

Figure 18.5 A composition set on the left-hand third

powerful we can see the force of the movement even in the simple graphic illustration. What do you think the audience would assume would be the next event? I think they would expect the dancers to twirl in the middle of frame. If this were to happen, then perhaps the central composition would be appropriate, but what do we cut to? This would, in fact, be an excellent end title shot.

Now let us look at Figure 18.5. Here the dancers' bodies are bisected by the left-hand third. There is a clear 'dynamic' input into the frame. Although their bodies are bisected by the left-hand third, the male partner's left (camera right) hand and foot extend beyond this portion of the frame.

There are now two influences on the frame – the balance of the frame is clearly created by the mass of the dancers' bodies, but there is a dynamic push to the right made by the male's extended limbs. So what does the audience conclude from this? That the woman is about to spin into the man's arms and they will dance to the right of the frame. Very much different to their conclusion from the composition in Figure 18.4.

Now let us put exactly the same couple, in exactly the same pose, in a composition where they are bisected by the right-hand third (Figure 18.6). What would the audience conclude from this composition? Something very different from the previous compositions.

What? Well, the balance is different but the shot has only changed by composing the couple on the right-hand third. What else? In the original pose the woman's right (camera left) hand had influence, but not of great magnitude; the man's left hand (camera right) had more influence but still not very significant.

In this composition the couple's camera right limbs become all-powerful in the dynamic of the frame. They actively and positively push the right-hand edge of the frame away from themselves. The audience's conclusion as to what is about to happen is therefore that they will now dance to the left, quite the reverse decision from when the same action was composed on the opposite side.

At this point it is well to remember that there is very little in the frame of a composition that doesn't have some influence on the audience.

Figure 18.6 A composition set on
the right-hand third

Figure 18.7 A composition set on
the lower sixth

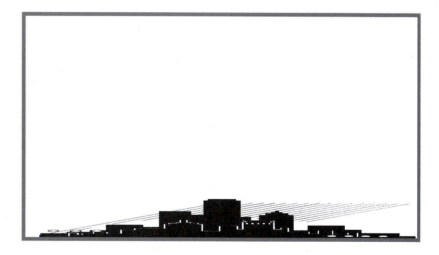

Framing using the sixths

Just as in music, in composition we too have the equivalent of the
minor chords. In the world of cinematography these are the lines of
the sixths – that is, any line one-sixth of the way in from any edge of
the frame or one-sixth of the frame width out from the centre of the
frame. The sixths coming out from the centre of the frame are very
weak in terms of compositional power, but those coming in from the
outside edge do have an appreciable power. Their power is far less
than the power of the thirds, but nevertheless it is a very useful compositional tool.

In Figure 18.7 the skyline is contained within the bottom sixth of
the frame. It makes a very pleasing composition, especially if in the
background there was, say, an attractive sunset. In fact, almost any
interesting object, on an important third or sixth, would, of course,
heighten the dramatic power of the composition. Leaving five-
sixths of the frame free causes this space to be very vulnerable in as

Figure 18.8 A composition using the upper and lower sixths

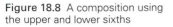

much as almost anything placed in that area will have an influence on the audience greater than its normal value in a less dramatic composition.

In this vacant space even the Red Baron is a powerful force! In Figure 18.8, by flying his aeroplane on the bottom line of the top left-hand sixth box, even in caricature, he is such a powerful compositional force that one's eye is totally distracted from the lovely skyline that previously dominated the frame. Such is the power of the sixths.

Diagonal framing

There are other elements within the frame that can have a very strong effect on the audience's response to the overall picture. Perhaps the next most powerful dynamic force within the frame is the diagonal line – that is, the line flowing directly from one corner of the frame to the diagonally opposite corner.

In Figure 18.9 there is a very simple composition of a cat looking at its master working at a painting. Study this composition. What is the cat looking at? There is little doubt, it's looking at the back of its master's head. Not at the painting. Not at the brush and not at the palette. But how can we be so certain that that is the cat's actual point of view?

Quite simply, the cat's eye-sockets are bisected by the bottom right to top left diagonal of the frame, as is the back of the painter's head. I have deliberately left out the eyes of both the cat and the painter to prove the point. Figure 18.10 is identical to Figure 18.9 but with the diagonal line inserted to show the path of its influence.

Complex and combined composition

It is also possible to compose individual elements of the overall picture within the separate nine boxes formed by the division of the frame by the lines of the thirds.

Figure 18.9 A composition using the diagonal

Figure 18.10 A composition showing the position of the diagonal

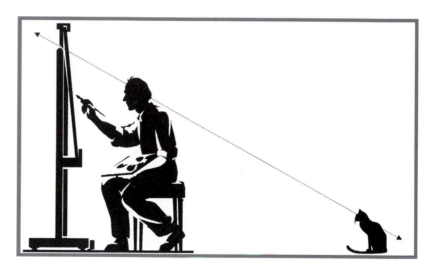

Figure 18.11 The effect of a 'weight' on a composition

Another variation is to combine different compositions within different elements of a single frame. Let us say that we are going to put a 'heavy' object within the right-hand vertical three boxes and a small, perhaps fragile, object in the bottom left-hand third box. If the subject looming in the right-hand third could be made to have an eyeline to the subject in the lower left-hand box, we would have a very effective composition.

Figure 18.11 is such a composition. The bear on the right is wholly composed within the right-hand third, while the butterfly is beautifully contained and composed within the lower left-hand third box. Here, combining at least two rules has given us an unusual and very effective composition. There are many, many variations on this, and other, themes.

19
Lenses and perspective

Frame size and focal length

Figure 19.1 represents a general view of a city scene. Marked on it are the framings for a wide-angle lens, a medium-angle lens and a medium close lens. As you can see, the different lenses only select different amounts of the scene. There is no change in perspective – none of the figures or items in the shot change their relationship to each other.

In Figure 19.2 you can see four more lens sizes – again there is no relational change between the elements of the scene in the different framings, even though the frame size has now changed radically.

In Figure 19.3 the framings for even more extreme long focal lengths are illustrated and again the relationships haven't changed.

Figure 19.1 A wide-angle, medium-angle and medium close view

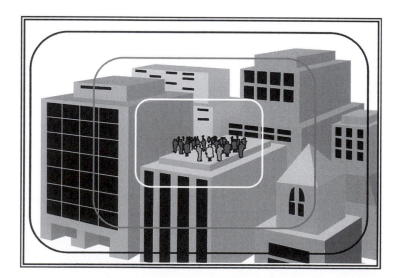

Figure 19.2 Close shots

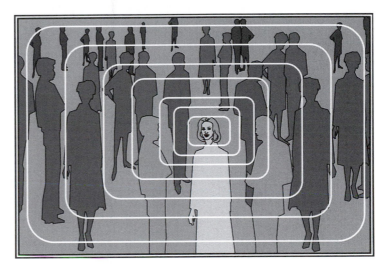

Figure 19.3 Long focal lens shots

If you were filming in Super 16, the widest framing in Figure 19.1 would perhaps be taken on a 9.5 mm lens and the tightest framing in Figure 19.3 would be at least a 500 mm lens.

What has happened is we have simply selected smaller and smaller segments of the original scene. Now, for the storytelling purposes of the film this might be just what we want, going closer and closer until we isolate the girl either within the middle of the scene, or even from the scene, thus concentrating the audience on that one person.

Perspective

Whereas in Figures 19.1–19.3 the camera was a very long way away from the subject and all the elements of the scene were relatively close

Figure 19.4 A wide shot on
Super 16 mm

Figure 19.5 Medium shot
on Super 16 mm

Figure 19.6 Close shot on
Super 16 mm

together, in Figure 19.4 there are three main elements in the scene and they are at very different distances from the camera.

The woman is quite close to the camera, indeed even in what is a wide shot of the background she is in a mid-shot. The car is in the middle distance and the houses are making the background. We can estimate that if the houses are 100 per cent of the scene depth away from the camera then the car is 60 per cent of the distance and the woman is perhaps 25 per cent.

This is quite different from Figures 19.1–19.3, where all the objects are within the range of 90–100 per cent of the camera to subject distance. So how do the elements of the scene behave as we use different lenses?

In Figure 19.5, where a middle-length lens has been used, the elements have grown in a slightly different ratio. This ratio is in proportion to their distance from the camera. The woman has grown in size considerably, the car a little and the houses only slightly.

In Figure 19.6, where an even longer lens would have been used, the woman has again grown, the car has disappeared completely and there is very little left of the houses.

How would this affect our reading of the script in each of these shots? In the wide shot (Figure 19.4), there is a very definite placing of the woman in an environment and the car is clearly a part of the action. In the medium close-up (Figure 19.5), the car might as well not be there and the woman is dominating the frame, but we are still aware of the environment (that is, the houses).

In Figure 19.6 the woman totally dominates the frame, the car is not present at all and the houses are having much less influence on what the picture, as a whole, is having on the audience.

So we can see that, without moving the camera, we can not only change the audience's attention by simply selecting the angle of view, but we can dramatically affect the audience's reaction to different elements of the scene by setting those elements at different distances from the camera before we select the area to be photographed.

In the sequence of Figures 19.4–19.6 we have not moved the camera – it stayed still and we changed lenses. In the sequence Figures 19.7–19.9 the lens remains the same but we move the camera to reframe on the woman.

In Figure 19.8 you can see what has happened. The three elements – the car, the houses and the woman – now look very different. The car is still playing in the story and we see far more of the houses, thus telling the audience a very different story. But the woman now dominates the frame.

What is the difference? In Figure 19.7 the three subjects stayed in the same relationship but in Figure 19.8 they have changed their relationship. The houses have moved from 100 per cent of the original distance to 95 per cent. The car has moved from originally 60 per cent to 52 per cent and the woman from 25 per cent to 15 per cent. So proportionally the woman has changed her relative distance from the camera more than the car and far more than the houses. Thus, the proportion of the frame that they occupy has changed in the same relationship.

This produces a very different reading of the overall picture by the audience. Both the car and the houses are still very much part of the scene.

If we now move the camera closer still and reframe to obtain the earlier close-up of the woman, the proportional relationship changes again.

Figure 19.7 Medium shot from same camera position

Figure 19.8 Medium shot using wider lens

Figure 19.9 Close-up using wide-angle lens

The houses are 90 per cent of the original distance, the car, say, 40 per cent and the woman now, say, 5 per cent of the scene depth in Figure 19.7.

What has happened? By comparison with the earlier close-up, things are very different. Again, we have a proportional change and again both the car and the houses are still in the story, so we are still discussing these elements of the scene with the audience.

One unfortunate thing has occurred, though. Carefully compare the close-ups in Figures 19.6 and 19.9. You will notice that the woman's face has become wider and a little distorted. This is a very common effect when taking a close-up on a wide-angle lens and should be guarded against. It must be handled very carefully and, if possible, should not be allowed to happen to the extent that a lay audience will ever notice it. Your actors and your producer, who has in all probability paid them large sums, will not thank you if you photograph them in this way.

But how has this distortion come about? It is simple – we have brought the camera so near that the proportional differences we discussed earlier now affect the contours of the face. At this distance, the camera is so close that the tip of the woman's nose is probably some 70 per cent of the distance to her ear lobes, so the proportional difference in size that affected the car and the houses is now sufficiently great as to affect the shape of her face.

Any lens wider than that considered normal for the format you are using should be avoided for a close-up. In fact, if at all possible, no close-up should ever be made on a lens less than twice the focal length of a normal lens.

So we see that we can never choose a lens for just its angle of view – the perspective that goes with that choice must always be considered.

Focal length and emotional involvement

Camera placement

It is important to remember that where you place your camera or, more exactly, where you place the nodal point of your taking lens is where you place your audience.

Think of it this way: the human eye is roughly spherical and when looking left or right, up or down, is rotating about the centre of that sphere as the eyeball swivels in the eye socket. With a camera lens, the optical centre of the lens, its nodal point, is the point where if you swivel the lens and camera about this point the image will appear to neither track left or right nor move up or down. Gears, and a few fluid heads, are constructed so that the pan and tilt movements can both rotate about the nodal point of the lens. When this is done the camera movements will be as close to the way a human eye rotates in its socket and therefore feel the most natural.

Extending this argument, it becomes clear that if we wish to either involve the audience in the action, or make it feel they are at a distance, where we figuratively place the centre of their eye will make them feel they are at that distance from the subject.

So choosing the camera position is very important, for it is also choosing the emotional position of the audience; this position will become the place they would physically expect to be observing from were they present, in real life, at the action to be photographed.

Keeping the audience at arm's length

If you look back at Figure 19.9, you can see an example of just how bad things can get if you are not acutely aware of the fact that, with your camera placement, you are transporting your audience. With very few exceptions, one would never take a camera this close to an artist. There is a common phrase of keeping something 'at arm's length' and this description has not come about by accident. We all have our physical space – that is, the actual area around our person that we would feel threatened if another person were to come inside it. For most of us it extends around us by an arm's length. If someone comes nearer to us than the stretch of our arm, we are going to feel threatened.

In Figure 19.9 the nodal point of the lens, and therefore your audience, must be around two feet or 50 centimetres from the woman's face. We have taken our audience within her physical space and are therefore asking either another protagonist in the script we are photographing that the camera is now playing or the audience itself to threaten the artist – something that should only be done intentionally, and rarely, and only when the script demands it.

Subjective and objective shots

Camera placement and the perspective created by your choice of focal length can seriously affect how the audience feels about their relationship with the scene. Figure 19.10 has been taken on a very-wide-angle lens; the impression this gives the audience is that they, or at least the person the camera is playing, are almost about to jump over the wall. They are highly involved with the action or positioning of the camera and the perspective conveys the idea of a dynamic movement into the garden and towards the house. This effect is described as

Figure 19.10 A wide-angle perspective

creating a subjective shot – that is, the camera, and therefore the audience, has become part of the subject, since their point of view is almost within the composition and the perspective is telling them the same thing.

If we now move on to Figure 19.11, things have changed somewhat. We are still using a wide-angle lens, but one having nothing like so extreme a wide-angle perspective. The shot width is roughly similar but the emotional positioning of the audience has changed. Although we can see roughly the same amount of information, the audience now has a feeling that, although they would clearly be seen from the house, they are not quite intruding on the privacy of its occupants. This is because the drawing power of the lens in use, which creates the perspective, has changed and this, together with the camera moving away from the house to get as wide a shot, has forced inclusion of the outer wall to the property; this has heightened both the physical, and more importantly, the emotional distancing, separating the audience from the scene.

Again, in Figure 19.12 we are maintaining roughly the same width of shot as far as the house is concerned, but have had to move further away again to achieve this. We now feel almost as if we are on a path, which indeed we are, and while we can see clearly into the garden we feel little emotional involvement with its occupants or anything that may be happening within. This is because we now have a perfectly normal perspective taken, not surprisingly, by what might be considered the normal focal length for a camera of this type. We have not forced either a subjective or an objective positioning of our audience. The relationship between subject and viewer is completely relaxed.

In Figure 19.13 we have moved back a little further while still trying to maintain the same width of shot. The effect is only subtly different from Figure 19.12, but can be important. By occluding the view of the

Figure 19.11 A less extreme wide angle

Figure 19.12 Shot with a
more 'normal' lens

Figure 19.13 A longer lens

terrace we have, in a certain way, made it more interesting, a little
more mysterious.

If we go back further still, and attempt to maintain the size of the
house in the frame, on this location we are forced to include some
branches in the foreground, thus giving the impression that the camera
is almost a 'peeping Tom' and is observing the house very much without
the occupant's permission, as in Figure 19.14. We have now reached
the focal length and therefore the perspective that makes this very

Figure 19.14 A medium
telephoto lens

Figure 19.15 A long
telephoto lens

much an objective or observational shot, very definitely not a subjective one.

Now let us consider what might happen if we take the camera still further away and put on a still longer focal length lens. Figure 19.15 is just this and now, simply by changing camera position and focal length of the lens, we are truly emotionally observational in our relationship with the house and its occupants. This is observational in the extreme, almost a surveillance shot.

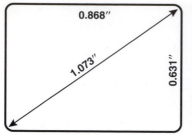

Figure 19.16   Calculating a 'normal' focal length lens for a given format size

What is a 'normal' focal length lens?

In all that has gone before in this chapter, we have been discussing the many and different effects on the image, perspective and emotions of our audience of our decision to choose a lens of one focal length or another. But is it possible to decide what is a 'normal' lens for any given format? It is very simple – the focal length of a 'normal' lens will be the same as the dimension on the diagonal of the frame format being used.

Therefore, for a standard Academy 35 mm frame the dimensions are as shown in Figure 19.16, though in this instance all the dimensions are specified in imperial measurements, i.e. inches. The diagonal comes out at 1.073 in. or as near as makes no difference a 25 mm lens.

20
Aspect ratios

The 35 mm frame

From the various originators of the motion picture camera came nearly as many ideas as to how a piece of movie film should be laid out, what the picture size should be and what type, if any, of perforations should be deployed. In 1907, an international agreement was reached stating that the film should be 35 mm wide, have a picture size of 0.980 in. × 0.735 in. and should have four perforations to each frame on both sides of the frame. This format is now referred to as a full aperture or as using an open gate. It is sometimes also referred to as the 'Silent' aperture. The layout of this format is shown in Figure 20.1.

It can only be imagined as to what negotiations were fought over to come to an agreement where the dimension of the frame was in inches (which both Britain and America use), the width of the film was measured in millimetres (a continental concept) and all the parameters of the perforation were totally American. Nevertheless, the standard was so perfect we are still using it as the main plank of our technology today.

With the coming of the sound on film, space had to be found for the optical soundtrack. The Society of Motion Picture Engineers of America standardized the required layout as one keeping the same relationship between the height and the width of the picture, but reducing the area by 24 per cent. As one side of the frame was to remain in the same place, this would leave room on the other side for the new soundtrack, as shown in Figure 20.2. This new picture size and placement is still known as the 'Academy' aperture and was formally standardized in February 1932.

As you can see in Figure 20.2, this had the added effect of widening the spaces between the frames. This was wasteful, but did come with one advantage – any need for mechanical joins could now be carried out within this new area and, for the first time, would not show to the audience.

Figure 20.1 Full-screen 35 mm 'Silent' aperture

Figure 20.2 The sound 'Academy' aperture

The aspect ratio

Many different screen shapes have evolved since the adoption of the Academy frame in 1932, but most have remained within the 35 mm four-perforation pull-down format. In order to readily describe these differing frames, we refer to them by their aspect ratio. The aspect ratio

177

is simply the mathematical relationship between the height and the width of the screen. It is always expressed with the height as 1. Therefore, if we divide the height of an Academy screen into its width and express the result in decimals we get 1.33, the width being 1.33 times the height. To be correct, an aspect ratio should always be shown with the 1 present and a ratio sign between it and the decimal, so an Academy frame becomes 1.33:1, which is said as 'one point three three to one'.

The joy of using an aspect ratio is that it matters not whether one is referring to a screen ratio or the aperture in the camera gate, the same figures will apply – so if a projectionist receives a tin marked as 1.33:1 they will know exactly how to present the film and in what format it is intended to be shown.

Figure 20.3 Viewfinder with 1.85:1, 1.66:1 and TV markings

Widescreen

The majority of feature films are currently shot in what is casually referred to as widescreen. This leads to some confusion as there are two, very similar, widescreen formats in use. In the USA, it is common to shoot widescreen in an aspect ratio of 1.85:1, while in mainland Europe 1.66:1 is more common. In Britain there is, most often, a typically British compromise. This entails using a 1.66:1 hard mask, the actual aperture cut into the camera gate, and marking up the viewfinder for both 1.66:1, the outer frame, and 1.85:1, which will be shown as two parallel lines just inside the top and bottom of the 1.66:1 markings. As so many features are pre-sold to television this is good practice, as slightly more emulsion area can be shown on television than could be cut from the 1.85:1 ratio. This is done by taking the television transfer, in 4 × 3 format, from the 1.66:1 master. A viewfinder showing all these requirements would appear as in Figure 20.3.

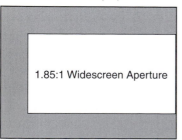

Figure 20.4 1.66:1 hard mask with 1.85:1 composition

This would translate to a camera negative layout as shown in Figure 20.4, where the outer rectangle is the 1.66:1 frame and the inner rectangle is the 1.85:1 frame. The frame bar between the individual frames has now grown even thicker. This wastage led to experiments with three-perforation pull-down, as discussed in the following section.

The area of emulsion now used by a 1.85:1 widescreen negative compared with the original full, or Silent, aperture is just 56 per cent of the original, as shown in Figure 20.5. It says a lot for the developments in emulsion technology that, despite using an image area of just a little over half the original, we think of today's screen images as being superb.

Figure 20.5 The 1.33:1 Academy aperture

Three-perforation pull-down

Some years ago, several manufacturers introduced 35 mm cameras either made for, or adaptable to, a three-perforation pull-down as against the traditional four. This was because it had been noted that a 1.85:1 negative picture could be accommodated in the height of three perforations if a hairline frame bar was accepted. The layout of the three-perforation format is shown in Figure 20.6. The purpose of introducing this was simply to reduce the cost of producing the master negative by 25 per cent.

Despite this being a very sound idea, which the camera manufacturers could easily go along with, editing equipment manufacturers were

Figure 20.6 Layout of three-perforation pull-down negative

less keen to rebuild their machines and the distributors, who run the cinemas, showed no interest at all in re-equipping the cinemas as this cost would far outweigh the saving in the cost of the print stock. As a result, any print struck from a three-perforation negative had to be optically printed up to a four-perforation print and the cost of this, compared to a straight contact print, outweighed the saving in negative cost.

Perhaps, as Super 16 mm had to wait, this too is an invention awaiting its time. As non-linear editing has done away with many rush prints in favour of a telecine transfer, and telecine machines can usually transfer three-perforation footage quite easily, we may yet see renewed interest in this format.

Three-perforation pull-down, some time later, became very popular in the USA, where many multi-episodic television shows are now shot on this format with specially constructed cameras utilizing 2000-foot magazines to enable long takes of continuous action to be achieved. On these shows, where by far the majority of the screen time is shot in a studio with three or four cameras, very like a live television studio, a print is never struck, for the camera negative goes straight to telecine and is edited and transmitted from this format.

It is interesting to note that, when utilizing 2000-foot magazines, the weight transfer caused by the film moving from the front of the magazine to the back is so great the tripod heads used are specially made with a lead screw under the camera mounting plate and a small handle at the back so that the operator can rebalance the camera during the shot.

In recent years, the introduction of digital intermediates (DI) – see Chapter 9 – has renewed interest in three-perf pull-down, for with this system the camera negative is scanned, just as for the TV shows, and all post-production is carried out in the digital domain. At the end of the post-production process, the images are simply played out via a digital to photomechanical printer but on to a four-perf master negative.

Two-perforation pull-down

Two-perf pull-down was very popular at one time, mainly in Italy, where Technicolor developed a system to enable 'spaghetti westerns' to be made on very low budgets. Some very well known films were made this way – *For a Few Dollars More*, etc. This frame layout is shown in Figure 20.7.

The problem, at the time, was that film stocks were nothing like as sophisticated as they are today and despite utilizing the full width of the old Silent frame, right out to the perforations and with no space for a soundtrack, the picture was never ideal. Although this was exactly the right aspect ratio for blowing up to 35 mm anamorphic print, unfortunately the quality of the projected image was noticeably inferior to one originated on a 35 mm negative using anamorphic lenses. The cost savings, though, were considerable, for while obtaining the same size and aspect ratio on the screen, half the original camera negative was used and there was no need to hire expensive anamorphic lenses.

Just as with three-perf pull-down, two-perf is having something of a renaissance. Using modern film stocks, high-quality modern lenses and DI post-production, very good looking prints can now be obtained.

Figure 20.7 Layout of two-perforation pull-down

This might mean more first time film-makers, and even film schools, could afford to shoot for anamorphic projection – an exciting thought.

Anamorphic

In order to give First World War tank drivers a better view, a French physicist, Henri Chretien, developed a lens system that was capable of expanding and compressing the horizontal angle of view. This developed into a single Hypergonar lens capable of being fitted to a film camera and a picture, *Construire un Feu*, was shot in France using just this one lens. By the beginning of the 1950s, American film-makers had come to the conclusion that providing cinemas with wider and wider screens was the answer to getting the audiences out of their houses and away from their television sets. In order not to increase costs appreciably, 20th Century Fox adopted and developed Chretien's principles to produce a range of lenses, of various focal lengths, capable of shooting a film in a convenient way, on conventional 35 mm film stock but with just a change of camera and cinema projector lenses. This resulted in an aspect ratio of well in access of 2:1. This system they named CinemaScope and it was very successful, being the first worldwide anamorphic process (*anamorphos* from the Greek *ana* = again, *morphos* = to form).

The horizontal compression of the CinemaScope format was 2:1. This gave CinemaScope an aspect ratio, when the 35 mm camera frame (0.868 in. $\times$ 0.631 in.) was expanded by the special lens, of 2.55:1. Pressure from the cinema owners caused this to be reduced to a standard of 2.35:1, mainly due to the architectural constraints of many existing cinemas; this was often reduced still further on showing, for the same reasons.

Figure 20.8 shows how the image is managed. The original scene is horizontally compressed by a ratio of 2:1 by the taking lens. This is then contact printed without any optical modification. When the print is shown in the cinema, the projector lens expands the image horizontally by the same ratio of 2:1 and the image is restored on the screen in the original height-to-width relationship.

In the early days of anamorphic photography, no compensation was made in the camera viewfinder and the operator had to compose the frame with the image compressed to half its actual width. Mercifully, most modern cameras capable of accepting anamorphic lenses can also be supplied with a de-anamorphosing viewfinder, so that the operator can view the image as the audience will see it. That the early operators could compose such wonderful images with a squeezed image fills me with admiration.

65 mm and 70 mm

In compressing and expanding the camera image with the anamorphic process, some horizontal definition is lost. To counteract this, several companies decided to shoot very wide screen pictures without a compression lens but using wider film. The Panavision company is probably the best known of the exponents of this format. Todd-AO,

Figure 20.8 The anamorphic
process

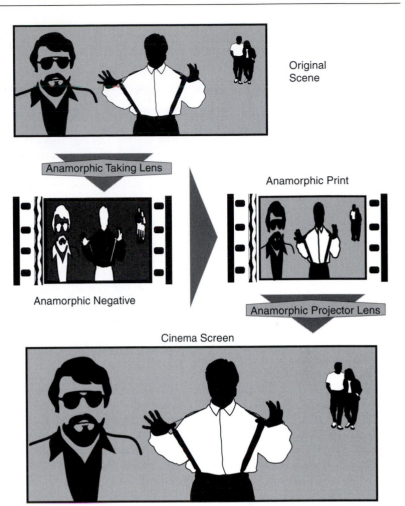

a name conjured from Richard Todd and the American Optical
Company who made lenses for him, must be a close contender. In both
these systems a 65 mm camera negative is employed using standard
35 mm perforations but utilizing five-perforation pull-down. With all
the other layout dimensions remaining similar to 35 mm and the image
going out to the perforations on both sides, no provision for sound is
made on the camera negative. This gives an image aspect ratio of
2.21:1. This aspect ratio is very close to CinemaScope's, but by utilizing
a far larger image area gives considerably improved image quality. It
also enables simple, spherical (non-anamorphic) lenses to be used.

In order to deliver sound to the cinemas, the 65 mm camera negative
is printed on to 70 mm wide print stock. So that the image can still be
contact printed, both films have their perforations, and images, in identical positions, the extra width coming as 2.5 mm outside each row of
perforations. This extra 5 mm of film accommodates the various sound
and control tracks. Figure 20.9 shows the layout of both the 65 mm
negative and the 70 mm print.

There are hybrid systems where, for reasons of origination cost, the
anamorphic process is used to make a 35 mm camera negative and this

Figure 20.9 The 65 mm negative
and a 70 mm print

65 mm Camera Negative

70 mm Release Print with Sound Tracks

is then optically expanded using a de-anamorphosing lens in the laboratory printer to produce a 70 mm release print. It is quite common for a film shot on a 35 mm anamorphic system to have a few release prints made on 70 mm for the premieres around the world and still make the majority of general release prints as 35 mm anamorphic prints. Clearly, this makes for a considerable cost saving.

It is also possible to take the reverse route and shoot on a 65 mm negative, make the premiere prints on 70 mm stock and still make the general release prints as 35 mm anamorphic prints, though the cost savings using this route are nothing like as great.

Super 35

This much-vaunted format, where you get a larger than Academy frame and can use existing spherical lenses, is effectively a return to the old Silent layout. With modern film stocks it is quite possible to print a 2.21:1 section from the middle of the frame and send it to the cinema either as a squeezed anamorphic print or enlarge it to 70 mm. The advantages in cost savings at the time of exposure are somewhat offset by the cost of optical printing to the delivery format.

For the camera operator, Super 35 can be a nightmare. In Figure 20.10 you can see what ought to be a simple two-shot, here composed correctly for the inner frame, which is 2.21:1. If, as many a producer may wish, another copy is struck for television, here shown by the larger rectangle with curved corners, the composition becomes a nonsense. The claim that you can shoot full frame and choose any aspect ratio later, from a compositional point of view, is clearly erroneous.

Figure 20.10 The layout of the Super 35 frame

Figure 20.11 CinemaScope
recomposed for 4 × 3 television

Television

Television started life as a competition between two systems, that of John Logie Baird, which had an upright or Portrait frame, and that from the Marconi Company, which displayed a horizontal, or View, frame. It was the Marconi system that was adopted with its horizontal aspect ratio of roughly 1.25:1. In 1952, the BBC changed this aspect ratio to 1.33:1 to conform with the then current cinema standard. More recently, with the advent of digitally transmitted television, the world is slowly going over to the latest standard, which is quoted as 16 × 9 (in cinema terms, 1.77:1). Although the 16 × 9 television format is closer to current widescreen cinema production, it does not conform to any existing standard and is a compromise, albeit, perhaps, a good one.

At some time or another, films made in all the formats previously discussed will come to be shown on television. Many will have been composed with this in mind as they will have funding from a television outlet built into the production budget. This may be all very well for the producer but it can be a nightmare for the operator, who may have to be thinking about several frame formats in the viewfinder all at the same time.

For big budget pictures this presents less of a problem, as funding should have been put aside for a pan and scan telecine transfer from a master copy to the television format of choice. Pan and scan involves a telecine operator moving a television-sized scanning area left and right across the widescreen frame to obtain the best possible composition out of the original framing. This is clearly not ideal, but is far better than just letting the television framing always be the centre section of the original widescreen frame.

If the film was originally shot in anamorphic, or 65 mm, the television frame section is likely to be a mere pastiche of the original concept. Figure 20.11 shows the 4 × 3 television aspect ratio overlaid on to a CinemaScope frame and Figure 20.12 shows the 16 × 9 ratio overlaid on to a CinemaScope frame. Both these recompositions make nonsense of the original framing. In Figure 20.11, the 4 × 3 version, three of the original four members of the cast have disappeared. In Figure 20.12, the 16 × 9 framing, the man on the left has managed to reintroduce his ear but the other two still remain virtually unknown to the television audience.

It is worth noting at this point that, while for over 60 years the film industry has referred to its aspect ratios as a ratio relative to unity, one,

Figure 20.12 CinemaScope recomposed for 16 × 9 television

Figure 20.13 The 1.66:1, 1.85:1 and the television 4 × 3 aspect ratios

Figure 20.14 The 1.66:1, 1.85:1 and the television 16 × 9 aspect ratios

the television industry has always referred to its aspect ratios as the nearest whole numbers representing height and width times each other.

Things are not quite as bad when taking a television scan from the centre section of a widescreen negative that has been shot with a 1.66:1 hard mask in the camera gate but was framed for theatrical release in the 1.85:1 aspect ratio. As we have seen, the television frame can be taken from the 1.66:1 frame, thus gaining both height and, more importantly, width of frame and getting nearer to the original composition. Figure 20.13 shows a 4 × 3 television frame overlaid on a 1.66:1 original, while Figure 20.14 shows the same but for a 16 × 9 television transfer.

The technique of shooting a negative in the ratio of 1.66:1 and taking the television frame from this whilst still intending to show the 1.85:1 frame in the cinema relies on the operator using a technique known as shoot and protect. This requires the camera operator to shoot the primary composition for 1.85:1 while protecting the 1.66:1 frame. Protecting, in this instance, means being absolutely certain that the 1.66:1 frame never shoots off the set, that microphones never intrude into this frame and nothing that does not relate to the story enters this, the outer, frame. The technique of shoot and protect is used in many other cross-format situations and, providing not too many formats are required, is not too arduous for the operator and can be very successful.

When shooting Super 16 mm for television, matters are a little complicated as the world has still not gone over completely to the 16×9 television format; therefore, within the frame, allowances may have to be made to accommodate a 16×9 composition, a 4×3 composition and even an interim format of 14×9 as used on UK analogue transmissions at present.

Part Five
The Future

21

Aspect ratios when shooting for television

The nature of the problem

There has been a problem in recent years as to how to 'future-proof' television programmes that might be transmitted in the old 4×3 aspect ratio but will, at some time, need to be repeated in the intermediate 14×9 aspect ratio or, eventually, in the 16×9 aspect ratio that has become the new international standard.

The whole argument should really be turned on its head, as both Super 16 mm film cameras and Digi Beta cameras happily shoot in an aspect ratio either exactly, or very close to, the 16×9 aspect ratio. Therefore, the true problem is 'now-proofing'. Most television programmes are almost all now originated in the 16×9 aspect ratio; therefore, the difficult decision is which compromise aspect ratio to transmit now on the gradually disappearing 4×3 standard.

It is interesting to look at the history of the 16 mm format, as this shows how the Super 16 mm standard, which was developed many years ago, has found its true value in recent years as an ideal format for shooting high-quality television; this is particularly true in the UK.

History – the evolution of the Super 16 mm format

In the early 1920s George Eastman, the founder of Kodak, together with the Bell & Howell company of Chicago, Illinois, set out to develop an amateur film standard, and a camera and projector to go with it. Bell & Howell favoured a 17.5 mm film, this being the standard 35 mm film simply slit in two. George Eastman objected strongly. He was adamant that a completely new standard was required because, up until then, the film base was nitrate and was very prone to bursting into flames. He was determined that the amateur film should only ever be available on the new 'Safety' film base and to ensure this there had to be a new standard. Eastman simply could not abide the idea of his new product being responsible for burning down a customer's home. Bell & Howell were not entirely happy, as one of their major patents was for the standard 35 mm sprocket hole, which would have been used again on 17.5 mm, though now only on one side of the film. George Eastman prevailed though, very much to our current benefit.

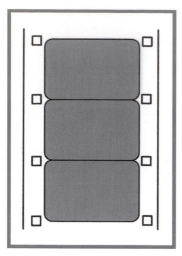

Figure 21.1 The 1923 silent 16 mm film layout

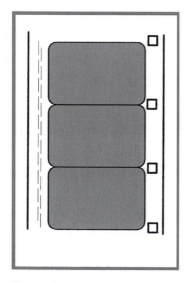

Figure 21.2 The 1932 standard 16 mm layout with a soundtrack

So Bell & Howell developed a new standard, a little narrower than 17.5 mm, and with a new, smaller, sprocket hole. There was also to be only two holes per frame, located either side of the film at the intersection of the frames and 16 mm wide, as shown in Figure 21.1 (35 mm has eight perforations per frame, four each side).

One of the design parameters of this development was that they had decided that, for amateur use, an image size of around one-sixth of the size of the silent 35 mm frame would be adequate.

In 1926, sound films came to the cinema. It wasn't long after that the now popular 16 mm amateur format also wanted sound. It was to be some time before the amateurs could record their own sound, but before this there was a market for feature films, cartoons, etc. to be shown at home. By now, the quality of 16 mm equipment, especially projector mechanisms, was such that it was apparent that they could give quite adequate image steadiness using only one row of perforations. In 1932, Bell & Howell introduced the Filmosound 120 projector, dispensing with the left-hand row of perforations and using this area for an optical soundtrack. The new format layout is illustrated in Figure 21.2. At this time the 16 mm standard was very much 'substandard' and, indeed, was often referred to by that name.

We now jump to the early 1960s, by which time 16 mm was almost semi-professional. In America much news film was being shot on the format, often using the Auricon camera or one of its derivatives. The soundtrack, for this application, was now on a magnetic strip coated down the left-hand edge where the optical track used to be.

Around the same time, the BBC in London was facing two problems. Firstly, they were about to open a second channel, BBC2, and both channels were about to go into colour. This was going to put up their filming costs considerably, for at that time drama was usually shot in 35 mm, though much of the factual output was then shot on 16 mm. They therefore decided that they would see if 16 mm could, at least for British television, become a truly professional gauge and the rest, as they say, is history.

The significance of the BBC's contribution to the development of 16 mm into a professional gauge should not be overlooked. Arthur Branson, and later Paul Bootle, put an enormous amount of energy and BBC resources into the huge improvements in the image quality of the 16 mm format. It is a wonderful synergy that as the BBC's throughput of 16 mm footage was so enormous, Kodak were prepared to fund considerable research and development to improve emulsions and the quality of the perforations, given that it was the founder of Kodak, George Eastman, who pushed for the gauge at its inception.

The BBC also provided funding, development resources and research for several of the then new self-blimped lightweight 16 mm cameras, as well as helping with the development of many of the high-speed prime lenses – setting the trend for many years to come in both 16 mm and 35 mm cinematography. They were also instrumental in developing and bringing to the market the new generation of relatively high-speed, long-range zoom lenses, which we now take for granted in 16 mm cinematography.

In the early 1960s there was another development that was, perhaps, to be just as significant in the history of 16 mm. Rune Erickson realized that if the 16 mm negative frame area was extended out to the edge currently occupied by the soundtrack, the resultant picture's

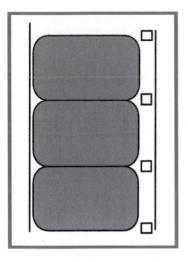

Figure 21.3 The Super 16 mm layout

aspect ratio would be very nearly the same as that used in most European feature films, i.e. 1.85:1. He therefore had the aperture of his Eclair NPR enlarged to very nearly the edge of the film, increasing the width of the frame by 2 mm, and thus inventing Super 16. His purpose was to reduce the negative cost of feature production in his native Scandinavia where, with such a small audience in the indigenous languages, production costs were of paramount importance. Figure 21.3 shows the frame layout of Erickson's new Super 16 format.

While his idea was practical, at the time there were some disadvantages. The negative emulsions were not anything like as good as they are today, the image was still far smaller than the 35 mm equivalent and with only one perforation per frame the mechanical stability of the gauge was inferior to 35 mm with its four perforations each side of every frame.

Despite the drawbacks, if treated with care, Super 16 was even then capable of a very impressive quality. You could not put a soundtrack on it since there was no space left, but this didn't matter, for in post-production the sound is always on a separate roll and for final presentation the negative was intended to be blown up to 35 mm, where there was room for the normal soundtrack.

Super 16 seemed to be a wonderful idea but it had not yet found its true place in the industry. In retrospect, it was a fabulous idea awaiting its time.

16 × 9 television and Super 16

We are now seeing the introduction of domestic 16 × 9 televisions; indeed, the majority in the shops, certainly in the UK, are now in this format. It seems likely that, in Europe at least, the standard for the new transmissions will be based on the current 625-line system but transmitted on a terrestrial, or satellite, digital system. The 16 × 9 aspect ratio is undoubtedly a compromise, but for Europe quite a good one. In the UK, we still shoot virtually most of our fictional television programmes on 16 mm, so Super 16 fits the 16 × 9 screen admirably. It is important to realize that most European feature films are shot on a 35 mm spherical lens format with an aspect ratio of 1.85:1, which again is very close to the proposed 16 × 9 television format, so European feature films will look very good on 16 × 9 television.

Despite a rearguard action by the ASC (American Society of Cinematographers), who would prefer a 2:1 widescreen television aspect ratio to conform with anamorphic production, which is the most common feature-film format in America, albeit being originated in the 2.35:1 aspect ratio, it does seem very probable that 16 × 9 will become a worldwide standard format, even if the transmission system varies from country to country. If this is the case, then Super 16 is an ideal format as its aspect ratio, as we have seen, is almost exactly the same. So, of course, is spherical 35 mm, which is more commonly used for US television.

At the moment, High Definition television seems too expensive for general domestic use in Europe, though the first station has recently gone on air. It is gaining considerable popularity elsewhere, particularly America and Japan.

The historical reasons for television coming into being with an aspect ratio of 4 × 3 are twofold. Firstly, it was the then cinema ratio – i.e. the Academy frame – devised by the Academy of Motion Picture Engineers of America when they had to change the full-frame 35 mm format to encompass a soundtrack. Secondly, when the Marconi electronic television system was adopted it was only possible to 'blow' the glass cathode ray tubes with the flat end circular. Therefore, the first, sensible, rectangle that could be contained within this circle had an aspect ratio of 4 × 3.

Let us not delude ourselves. The current push to change the aspect ratio of home televisions from the original worldwide standard of 4 × 3 (1.33:1) up to 16 × 9 (1.77:1) is predominantly to enable the manufacturers to sell more televisions, the market having deemed to be saturated with 4 × 3 colour televisions. So give them something new to buy – widescreen! One can't help remembering how, in the 1950s, the same approach was applied to cinema to try to counteract the growth of television.

As a cinematographer, I am delighted – 16 × 9 is a much better frame within which to compose and Super 16, in this format, gives much improved image quality.

There are a number of matters that have to be taken on board, though. The secret of successfully producing a Super 16 film for television has to be forward planning. There are many pitfalls in the use of this gauge, though these can easily be overcome with foresight. For instance:

1   Not all the lenses we are used to using cover Super 16.
2   There is only one camera available that will run backwards.
3   At present there are no stunt cameras in Super 16, i.e. gun cameras.
4   Are you going to edit on a non-linear computer-based program such as Avid or even Final Cut Pro? If not, do you have a Super 16 Steinbeck?
5   How are you going to deliver the product – 16 × 9 videotape or 4 × 3 videotape – and in what format?
6   Does your commissioning editor want both 4 × 3 and 16 × 9 versions?
7   Do you need a projection copy for festival showing? If so, how do you get a soundtrack on to it?

Note that, because of all the different delivery options, you must give the laboratory much more information than on a Standard 16 production.

Framing in several formats

Perhaps the greatest problem for the camera department is not Super 16 equipment, or even Digi Beta or High Definition – there is plenty available for most jobs – but how to compose the picture. It doesn't sound like a difficult problem, does it? Well, here is one edict from a major UK television station for a Super 16 project (I paraphrase a little):

The master negative shall be Super 16 clean of all extraneous objects such as microphones and shall not shoot off the set. If you are making a drama then, on analogue terrestrial television, you may transmit in 14 × 9 with a small letterbox but not 16 × 9. You will be able to transmit in 16 × 9 only on a terrestrial digital station. You will also be required to provide a full-screen 4 × 3 version for foreign sales.

Similar clauses are inserted in contracts for Digi Beta and HD productions.

Figure 21.4 A well-composed
16 × 9 frame

Figure 21.5 A 14 × 9 section
from the middle of a 16 × 9
frame

Let us take some examples to demonstrate the problem. In
Figure 21.4 we have a well-composed 16 × 9 scene – the cloisters of a
university with two undergraduates shaking hands on the right-hand
side of the frame.

Over this I have shown a 16 × 9 or Super 16 frame. All is well at
this point and we have a very nice composition with a good dynamic
composition.

If we now recompose the centre section, as is the norm, for 14 × 9,
we see – in Figure 21.5 – just what we would be transmitting. It really
is not acceptable. One undergraduate has nearly disappeared out of
the right-hand side of the frame and no one in their right mind would
have made an original composition in this way. I am sure, though,
there would be many non-production executives who would find this
acceptable if only because the cost of pan and scanning the original to
correct the composition would, in their eyes, be prohibitive.

Figure 21.6 A 4 × 3 section from
the middle of a 16 × 9 frame

But now let us look at what the purchasers of the programme for
viewing abroad have to put up with. In Figure 21.6 I have shown the
same scene with the 4 × 3 centre section recomposed. One undergraduate has now completely disappeared.

This really is a ridiculous situation. If we were to frame the original
for 4 × 3, then the 14 × 9 UK transmission will lose all the power of the
frame and in a 16 × 9 frame there will be no dynamic to the frame at all,
as the two undergraduates will now be very nearly in the middle of the
frame, a very boring composition. Do we really want to descend to this
level of artistry in the name of future-proofing? Our real problem, at
least until 16 × 9 televisions take over completely, is 'now-proofing'.

Here I must make a plea to the production office. Let us imagine
you have had your initial transmission and you are sitting back review-
ing your great success. A call comes from the foreign sales department
and you order a 4 × 3 copy. Seems simple, doesn't it? Now without
further information your telecine operator is quite likely to assume
you mean the old 4 × 3 and put it up on a Standard 16 telecine. It's not
his fault, and please don't shout at him – you should have asked for
Centre Section Super 16 transfer to 4 × 3.

If you don't, then the result will be as in Figure 21.7, since he will clip
off the left-hand side of the film – the right-hand side of the screen –
and both undergraduates vanish!

Framing solutions

If you are lucky enough to be shooting for the UK Channel 4, then you
are very fortunate. They currently are quite happy to transmit drama
in true 16 × 9, even on their whole output – with the appropriate
letterbox – and are heavily committed to the future of a European
16 × 9 format. In fact, they seem to be the only channel so totally committed on any analogue station in the UK.

When shooting for many stations across the world you have to deliver
in three formats. The current position in the UK seems to be that they

Figure 21.7 A 4 × 3 Standard 17 telecine transfer from a Super 16 negative

Figure 21.8 An 'ideal' 14 × 9 composition

assume fiction will be transmitted 14 × 9, but might be persuaded to transmit 16 × 9. It is important to recognize the word 'deliver' – things will change as the UK goes over to digital 16 × 9; only then will we be allowed to truly realize the artistic potential of the 16 × 9 format.

The important thing, therefore, is to establish in what aspect ratio your primary transmission will be and in what other aspect ratios you must deliver, and come to an agreed compromise before you start shooting. A change of mind later can be both unpleasant to look at and very expensive.

My own position is that I would prefer to make the best composition for the primary transmission format – if this were 14 × 9, then the composition would now look like Figure 21.8. But I would ask for a budget to make a pan and scan transfer to any narrower format. I

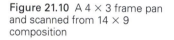

Figure 21.9 A 14 × 9 composition on a 16 × 9 frame with 4 × 3 frame pan and scanned

Figure 21.10 A 4 × 3 frame pan and scanned from 14 × 9 composition

also make every effort to ensure that I attend that transfer. Figure 21.9 shows how 16 × 9, 14 × 9 and 4 × 3 would look using this principle.

Therefore, if this composition were later transmitted on a full format 16 × 9 system, then it would look like the white outline in Figure 21.9. Not fantastic, but very acceptable, for putting the undergraduates on the edge of this frame, as in Figure 21.6, has more impact. The mid-grey outline is the primary composition; 14 × 9 and the light grey outline would be the pan and scan 4 × 3 version, also very acceptable.

Without pan and scan the foreign sales version would look like Figure 21.10 – which is still unacceptable.

On the other hand, let us assume that the producers have retained sufficient funds for a pan and scan transfer and have invited the cinematographer to supervise it. What a difference this would make. Any foreign purchaser would not only be pleased with the framing of

Figure 21.11 A 4 × 3 pan and scan composition from a 16 × 9 image originally composed for 14 × 9

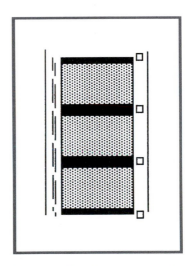

Figure 21.12 A 16 mm combined optical print with 1.85:1 reduction mask

Figure 21.11, but would never know it had been shot on any other format. Such is the power of forward planning.

Festival prints

Now let us consider the problem of showing your work at festivals, and I am all for this – we all like to receive awards.

Most festivals can only show 16 mm as a Standard ComOpt print, i.e. Standard 16 with a combined optical track, as in Figure 21.12. There are a very few festivals that can show a Super 16 print with its SepMag, separate magnetic track, on a separate roll.

You have several options. You could make a centre section 4 × 3 print, but we have seen how this can ruin both the composition and the pace of the editing – which means you are unlikely to win that award. You could make a 35 mm print, since all festivals can show them, and it may increase your chances of winning, but it is very expensive. You could show your work on videotape – on the other hand, that is probably a bad idea.

There is one very good option, though. This is to have the full Super 16 frame reduction printed so that the width is reduced to the Standard 16 frame width and the leftover area top and bottom of the frame printed in black, as in Figure 21.12.

This is an excellent option, since the grain structure of the print stock is so fine that when projected it will look very nearly as good as a Super 16 print. The only problem is that when it is shown it will seem a small frame, vertically, compared with Standard 16. If you can have a word with the projectionist and persuade him to put a wider angle lens on the projector and try and fill the screen he would use for a 35 mm 1.85:1 screening, you will be surprised how well the image looks.

Alternatively, if you have the money, scanning your Super 16 negative into a digital interface file and printing out on an Arri laser printer can deliver truly superb images, as described earlier in this book.

22
High Definition – HD

Is film dead?

No, most certainly not!

Over the past few years I have been closely connected with the introduction of HD and, while I believe the pictures can be wonderful, the reasons for choosing to shoot with HD, as opposed to film, are not as numerous as it first appeared.

Three-chip cameras

The first wave of HD cameras with their three-chip configuration were, and indeed still are, able to emulate the quality of image obtainable when using 35 mm film, but only if you used the finest lenses. Many so-called HD lenses produced a picture nowhere near the camera's capability, which caused the cameras to get a mixed reception. Those that saw demonstration films shot with top quality lenses, such as Panavision's, were usually impressed and those that saw material from poorer glass were usually disappointed.

In some areas the HD three-chip format was very successful. For instance, within three years of the introduction of HD, nearly half the multi-episodic, multi-camera shoots for US television were shot using HD. Here the attraction is clear, with quality virtually the same as the three-perforation pull-down 35 mm cameras that have traditionally been used to shoot these shows, and recording medium costing around one-fortieth the price (yes, 1/40!), the sums really worked in HD's favour.

Star Wars – Attack of the Clones, the first full-length feature film shot on HD – looked very good indeed. Photographed by David Tattersall BSC, I could hardly tell if I was watching a mechanically projected print or a digitally projected image, and both versions were excellent. George Lucas, it is said, prefers the digital version. But why shoot a picture costing over $1 000 000 on HD? Surely not to save money – no, here the advantage was the ability to go straight from the camera master image directly to the computers that would be used for the huge amount of image post-production without leaving the digital domain. The need to carry out a lot of digital post-production is a powerful argument for originating on HD.

Single-chip cameras

Matters have moved forward and several manufacturers have introduced single-chip cameras, where the chip is approximately the size of the frame used in 35 mm photography and some of them have, effectively, twice the resolution of the first generation three-chip cameras. Perhaps the greatest advantage of these cameras is their use of exactly the same lenses as 35 mm film cameras. It remains to be seen if these cameras will increase the popularity of shooting feature films in the digital format.

Digital presentation

There are clear financial advantages for the distributors of feature films if cinemas are equipped with digital projectors of sufficient quality such that the audience are unaware of the change from mechanical to digital projectors. The savings come in some surprising places. In the distribution chain, it is said that the cost of transporting film prints, i.e. vans etc., from theatre to theatre is more than the cost of producing the prints themselves. If this is the case, were it possible to deliver the virtual digital image by, say, fibre-optic or satellite, a large cost of delivering the images to the cinema would be saved.

The other side of the distribution dilemma is interesting, as the distributors do not own the projectors: the exhibitors own the cinemas and the projectors, so the cost of conversion would fall on the shoulders of the exhibitors, who are unlikely to make any extra profit from the change-over. Currently, the comparable price of a digital projector able to give a picture of comparable quality to a mechanical projector is substantial, an HD projector costing some three times as much as the mechanical equivalent.

Conclusions

HD digital cinema, I believe, is bound to come but I suspect slowly, as there are many obstacles to overcome, though few of these are of a technical nature – all the required delivery systems and projection equipment are available today. It will need an important agreement between the distributors and the exhibitors for the revolution to happen.

There will be some films that will cry out to be shot in the digital HD format and others that will not. Futuristic and hyper-realistic movies, together with those requiring a lot of digital post-production, will be well suited to HD, though I believe that for many years to come the more human story-based movies will still shoot on film. Why? Because there is over 100 years of history and knowledge in how to stir the emotions of an audience, via their eyes, that lies vested in that peculiar controlled rotting of silver. We Directors of Photography have been successfully giving our audience pictures they love, and know how to emote to, on film for those 100 years or so – long may it continue.

Index

Also available from Focal Press

High Definition and 24P Cinematography

Paul Wheeler

'A welcome addition to his two previous books...providing an extremely comprehensive and valuable introduction...Wheeler's enthusiasm for HD is refreshingly uncomplicated...This is an excellent book.'

Zerb, *Journal of the Guild of Television Cameramen*

This authoritative new reference demystifies the technologies of high definition and 24P cinematography. It is written for the director of photography, camera crew and producer or director and deals with the subject from their point of view. It provides a thorough and logical description of the five scanning formats 24P, 25P, 30P, 50i and 60i as well as recording formats, editing options, delivery potential and discussions on the financial implications these decisions might have.

High Definition and 24P Cinematography is filled with practical advice for tackling everyday decisions and choices, this is a must-have guide for anyone using or considering using high definition technology.

Paul Wheeler was trained at the BBC rising to become a Senior Drama Film Cameraman. A renowned cinematographer/director of photography, and previous Head of Cinematography at the National Film & Television School where he still runs courses on Digital Cinematography. Previous Head of Cinematography on the Royal College of Arts MA course. Twice nominated by BAFTA for a Best Cinematography award and twice winner of the INDIE award for Best Digital Cinematography.

March 2003: 189 × 246 mm: 100 illustrations: Paperback: 0 240 51676 1.

To order your copy call +44 (0)1865 474010 (UK) or +1 800 545 2522 (USA) or visit the Focal Press website: www.focalpress.com.

Also available from Focal Press

Cinematography

Image Making for
Cinematographers,
Directors and Videographers
Blain Brown

'A gorgeous piece of work that
bids to become a classic text on
cinematography .... Few books on
cinematography meld aesthetics
and pragmatics as deftly as this
one.'
American Cinematographer

- The definitive guide to
  cinematography
- Up-to-date coverage of
  technical topics, including High
  Definition and digital imaging
- Beautifully illustrated throughout to bring issues of color and light
  to life

Lavishly produced and illustrated, *Cinematography* covers the entire
range of the profession. The book is not just a comprehensive guide
to current professional practice; it goes beyond to explain the theory
behind the practice, so you understand how the rules came about
and when it's appropriate to break them. In addition, directors will
benefit from the book's focus on the body of knowledge they should
share with their Director of Photography.

Blain Brown was educated at CW Post College; MIT and Harvard
Graduate School of Design. He has completed projects as a director,
editor and screenwriter; with three screenplays produced. He has
also taught courses in storytelling and visual communication. As a
Director of Photography specializing in features and commercials, he
is now based in Los Angeles. His books include *A Sense of Place;
Motion Picture* and *Video Lighting* and *The Filmmaker's Pocket
Reference*. His work can be seen at www.BlainBrown.com.

October 2002: 189 × 246 mm: 450 colour illustrations: Paperback:
0 240 80500 3.

To order your copy call +44 (0)1865 474010 (UK) or +1 800 545 2522
(USA) or visit the Focal Press website: www.focalpress.com.

Focal Press   www.focalpress.com

Join Focal Press online

As a member you will enjoy the following benefits:

- browse our full list of books available
- view sample chapters
- order securely online

Focal eNews

Register for eNews, the regular email service from Focal Press, to receive:

- advance news of our latest publications
- exclusive articles written by our authors
- related event information
- free sample chapters
- information about special offers

Go to www.focalpress.com to register and the eNews bulletin will soon be arriving on your desktop!

If you require any further information about the eNews or www.focalpress.com please contact:

USA	**Europe and rest of world**
Tricia Geswell	Lucy Lomas-Walker
Email: t.geswell@elsevier.com	Email: l.lomas@elsevier.com
Tel: +1 781 313 4739	Tel: +44 (0) 1865 314438

Catalogue

For information on all Focal Press titles, our full catalogue is available online at www.focalpress.com, alternatively you can contact us for a free printed version:

USA	**Europe and rest of world**
Email: c.degon@elsevier.com	Email: j.blackford@elsevier.com
Tel: +1 781 313 4721	Tel: +44 (0) 1865 314220

Potential authors

If you have an idea for a book, please get in touch:

USA	**Europe and rest of world**
editors@focalpress.com	ge.kennedy@elsevier.com